AF436861

Buzzing with Magic: Quick & Effective Witchcraft for Busy Bees

Emilee Avink

Published by Emilee Avink, 2024.

While every precaution has been taken in the preparation of this book, the publisher assumes no responsibility for errors or omissions, or for damages resulting from the use of the information contained herein.

BUZZING WITH MAGIC: QUICK & EFFECTIVE WITCHCRAFT FOR BUSY BEES

First edition. May 24, 2024.

Copyright © 2024 Emilee Avink.

ISBN: 979-8223311713

Written by Emilee Avink.

Also by Emilee Avink

Embracing the Witch's Shadow: A Guide to Transformation and Self-Discovery: Unlocking the Secrets of Witchcraft, Healing and Personal Empowerment

Where Two Worlds Collide

The Infinite Loop: A Time Traveler's Search for Love

Whispers of the Guardian: Haleema's Legacy

The Pot of Plenty: Stretching Your Dollar with 50 Delicious Rice and Bean Dishes

Description for Nine Lives of Magic: Working with Your Feline Familiar

Once Upon a Feast: Fairytale Treats for Little Chefs

The Glitching Grimoire: A Tech Witch's Guide to Digital Spellcraft

The Healing Table: Crystal-Infused Meals

Buzzing with Magic: Quick & Effective Witchcraft for Busy Bees

The Witch's Daily Cup: Rituals and Recipes for Coffee Magic

Copyright © 2024 Emilee Avink
All rights reserved.
Printed by KDP in the USA.

BUZZING WITH MAGIC: Quick & Effective Witchcraft for Busy Bees.....................

Calling All Stressed Witches: Reclaim Your Magic with Busy Bee Witchcraft!.............

Part 1: The Busy Bee Witch Mindset - Reframing Magic for Your Life...................

Chapter 1: Reframing Your Perception of Magic - Unveiling the Magic in the Mundane.....

Chapter 2: Time Management for the Magically Inclined - Mastering Your Schedule with a Touch of Magic......

Part 2: Magic for Every Moment - Weaving Enchantment into Your Busy Bee Life.........

Chapter 3: Morning Buzz: Starting Your Day with Intention...........................

Chapter 4: Noon Nirvana: Magical Lunch Break Hacks............................

Chapter 5: Evening Enchantment: Winding Down After a Busy Day....................

Part 3: Maintaining Your Magical Practice - Busy Bee Style...........................

Chapter 6: Moon Magic on the Move: Fitting Lunar Work into Your Busy Life.............

Chapter 7: Short and Sweet Sabbat Celebrations.....................................

Chapter 8: Building Your Busy Bee Coven..

Part 4: Expanding the Magical Toolkit - Busy Bee Edition..............................

Chapter 9: Everyday Magic: Weaving Spells into Your Day...........................

Chapter 10: Tech Magic: Your Digital Grimoire....................................

Chapter 11: Busy Bee Travel Magic: Taking Your Practice on the Go...................

Part 5: Deepening the Connection with Nature - A Busy Bee's Guide...................

Chapter 12: Busy Bee Gardening Magic: Herbs & Flowers for Everyday Spells...........

Beyond the Basics: Herbal Incenses and Culinary Craft:..............................

Chapter 13: Busy Bee Nature Connection: Finding Magic in Every Moment..............

Part 6: Busy Bee Magic for Modern Challenges.....................................

Chapter 14: Busy Bee Stress Management: Magical Tools for Peace...................

Chapter 15: Busy Bee Self-Care Magic: Rejuvenating Your Spirit....................

Bonus Content: More For Your Busy Bee Witch Toolkit..............................

Glossary of Busy Bee Witchcraft Terms:...

Sample Busy Bee Weekly Schedule:..

Printable Spell Cards: Create Your Own Busy Bee Witch Arsenal!......................

Buzzing with Magic: Quick & Effective Witchcraft for Busy Bees

Calling All Stressed Witches: Reclaim Your Magic with Busy Bee Witchcraft!

Do you ever find yourself gazing longingly at your forgotten athame or neglected Book of Shadows, yearning for the days when witchcraft wasn't a luxury reserved for stolen moments in the moonlight? Let's face it, the modern world throws everything it has at us. The alarm clock screams, demanding our attention from sunrise to sunset, leaving us utterly spent by the time we collapse into bed. The idea of squeezing in a full moon ritual or brewing a complex potion feels like a distant fantasy.

But here's the empowering truth, dear witch: you don't have to abandon your magical practice! This book is your secret weapon, a guide to becoming a **Busy Bee Witch** – a powerful practitioner who thrives amidst the whirlwind. Forget the misconception that witchcraft requires hours of chanting under the full moon or complicated ceremonies involving exotic ingredients. We'll show you how to transform your everyday routine into a magical tapestry, infusing it with intention, wonder, and a sprinkle of practical magic.

In Busy Bee Witchcraft, you'll discover:

- **The Magic Mindset Shift:** We'll help you reframe your perception of witchcraft. It's more than just spells and rituals. It's about cultivating a sense of wonder and injecting mindfulness into the seemingly mundane tasks that fill your day. From grocery shopping to commuting, we'll help you discover the magic already present in your life, waiting to be unlocked.

● **Time-Management Mastery for Magical Bees:** Busy schedules are a reality, and this book gets it. We'll equip you with powerful time-management techniques specifically tailored for the magical practitioner. Learn to prioritize effectively, create a realistic and magical schedule that integrates seamlessly into your life, and even discover a few time-management spells and visualizations to boost your productivity.

This book is more than just words on a page; it's your key to reclaiming your magic, even amidst the chaos. So grab your metaphorical wand (or your trusty coffee stirrer, we won't judge!), and get ready to weave the extraordinary into your busy life. We'll show you how to be a Busy Bee Witch – a magical being who buzzes with the power to transform the everyday into the extraordinary.

Busy Bee Witchcraft offers options to fit your unique practice:

● **Are you a solitary practitioner yearning for connection?** We'll explore ways to build a virtual coven or cultivate a sense of community even when flying solo.

● **Do you crave a deeper connection with nature?** We'll show you how to incorporate nature magic into your daily routine, even if you live in a concrete jungle.

● **Does technology intimidate you, or are you curious about its potential?** We'll delve into the exciting world of digital grimoires and explore apps that can enhance your practice.

No matter your background or experience level, Busy Bee Witchcraft empowers you to create a magical practice that thrives alongside your busy life.

Part 1: The Busy Bee Witch Mindset - Reframing Magic for Your Life

Being a busy bee witch isn't about having oceans of free time or a life dedicated solely to elaborate rituals. It's about cultivating a magical mindset that allows you to weave the essence of witchcraft into the very fabric of your everyday life, even amidst the constant buzz. This first part explores this core concept, equipping you with the tools to reframe your perception of magic and make it work for you.

Many newcomers to witchcraft might envision a world filled with elaborate rituals, exotic ingredients requiring international shipping, and hours spent chanting under the light of a perfectly full moon. While these practices certainly have their place and beauty, busy bee witches embrace a more practical and integrated approach. Here's how to shift your perspective and discover the magic that's already there:

Magic as a Lifestyle, Not Just Spells and Rituals: Witchcraft is more than just casting spells; it's a way of being present and intentional in the world around you. It's about connecting with nature, harnessing the power of intention, and cultivating a sense of wonder in the everyday world, even the seemingly mundane. Look for opportunities to infuse magic into your daily routine – from setting mindful intentions as you brew your morning coffee to appreciating the beauty of a blooming flower on your way to work. Perhaps you can keep a crystal in your pocket for a touch of grounding energy during a stressful meeting, or listen to uplifting music during your commute to raise your vibrations and set the tone for a productive day.

Identifying the Magic Already Present in Your Daily Routine: Take a moment to reflect on the magic already present in your daily activities. Cooking a meal becomes a transformative act, nourishing your body and fueling your magical practice. Cleaning your home becomes a ritual of purification, clearing away negativity and creating a space that reflects your intentions. Even the act of commuting can be infused with magic – listen to uplifting music to raise your vibrations or visualize a protective shield around you as you navigate the hustle and bustle. Perhaps you can see your daily tasks as opportunities to practice mindfulness, focusing on the present moment and appreciating the small details.

Cultivating Gratitude for the Small Things: Gratitude is a powerful magical tool. By appreciating the small blessings in your life, you amplify their positive energy and attract more abundance. Take a moment each day to acknowledge the things you're grateful for – a supportive friend, a sunny day, a delicious meal. Feeling grateful raises your vibration and allows you to connect with the magic that surrounds you. It can be as simple as keeping a gratitude journal or taking a few minutes each morning to silently appreciate the things that bring you joy.

Busy Bee Witchcraft: Options to Fit Your Unique Practice:

- **Do you crave a deeper connection with nature?** We'll show you how to incorporate nature magic into your daily routine, even if you live in a concrete jungle. Perhaps you can keep a small potted plant on your desk or windowsill, or take a mindful walk during your lunch break to connect with the energy of the trees.

- **Does technology intimidate you, or are you curious about its potential?** We'll delve into the exciting world of digital grimoires and explore apps that can enhance your practice. Maybe you can use a meditation app to find moments of peace in your busy day or create a digital altar on your phone or tablet.

- **Are you a solitary practitioner yearning for connection?** We'll explore ways to build a virtual coven or cultivate a sense of community even when flying solo. Perhaps you can join online forums or social media groups to connect with other witches or find a pen pal who shares your interests.

Part 2 will delve into the art of time management for busy bee witches, ensuring your magical practice thrives alongside your demanding schedule.

Chapter 1: Reframing Your Perception of Magic - Unveiling the Magic in the Mundane

Ever feel like magic is a luxury reserved for those with hours to spare, lounging in robes and stirring bubbling cauldrons? Like spells and rituals are elaborate affairs that simply don't fit into your jam-packed schedule? Well, busy bee witch, it's time to rewrite that narrative! This chapter is all about shattering the misconception that witchcraft requires a life of incense-burning and cauldron-stirring. We'll explore how to integrate magic into your everyday routine, transforming the seemingly mundane into a tapestry woven with intention and wonder.

Magic as a Way of Being:

Let's move beyond the idea of magic as a fleeting act and instead embrace it as a way of living and breathing. It's not just about casting spells or performing elaborate rituals under the full moon (although those can be powerful too!). It's a way of viewing the world with a sense of awe and recognizing the interconnectedness of all things. It's about fostering a sense of wonder in the ordinary and infusing your daily life with intention.

Options to Personalize Your Magic:

• **The Coffee Connoisseur Witch:** Imagine this: instead of mindlessly brewing a cup of coffee to jolt you awake, you can transform it into a simple yet magical morning ritual. As you grind the beans, focus on your intentions for the day. Breathe in the rich aroma, letting it invigorate you. Pour the hot water over the grounds, visualizing your goals taking shape. Voila! You've just incorporated a magical element into your morning routine, setting your intentions for a productive day. This small act of mindfulness elevates your coffee from a simple beverage to a tool for manifestation.

- **The Tech-Savvy Witch:** Perhaps you're not a coffee person, but rely on a morning smoothie to kickstart your day. Maybe you can use a meditation app to find moments of peace in your busy day, focusing on your intentions for the day as the calming sounds wash over you. Create a digital altar on your phone or tablet, featuring images or symbols that resonate with your practice and intentions.

Finding the Magic Already There:

Look closely at your daily routine. Magic isn't some mythical creature hiding in the shadows; it's woven into the fabric of your everyday life, waiting to be discovered. The rhythmic sound of rain on your windowpane can be a soothing white noise lullaby, or the way sunlight dances on your morning toast can be a reminder of the warmth and life force that energizes the world. Here are some ways to tap into the magic already present:

- **The Nature Enthusiast Witch:** Perhaps you take a mindful walk during your lunch break, focusing on the intricate details of a blooming flower or the majestic form of a tree. That's a magical connection right there! By opening your eyes (and other senses) to the beauty and wonder surrounding you, you tap into the inherent magic of the natural world. Even if you live in a concrete jungle, consider keeping a small potted plant on your desk or windowsill as a reminder of nature's power.

- **The Urban Explorer Witch:** Maybe your commute is your connection to nature. Notice the intricate dance of city life - the way traffic patterns resemble a swirling vortex, or the hum of a busy street transforming into a vibrant song of human energy. By recognizing the magic in the seemingly mundane, you elevate your everyday experiences and cultivate a sense of wonder that fuels your witchcraft.

The Power of Gratitude as a Magical Amplifier:

Cultivating gratitude is a powerful magical tool often overlooked in the quest for grand spells and rituals. By appreciating the small things, you not only enhance your happiness but also magnify the magic already present in your life. Start a gratitude journal, listing down things you're thankful for, from a delicious cup of tea to the support of loved ones. This simple act of acknowledging blessings amplifies their energy, attracting more positivity into your life.

Think of gratitude as a magical fertilizer; the more you nourish your appreciation for the good things, the more magic blossoms and thrives in your world. Gratitude unlocks a deeper connection to the present moment, allowing you to savor the magic already infused in your daily experiences. A rushed commute becomes an opportunity to appreciate the intricate dance of city life, the synchronized flow of traffic lights becoming a mesmerizing spell cast upon the urban landscape. By recognizing the magic in the seemingly mundane, you elevate your everyday experiences and cultivate a sense of wonder that fuels your witchcraft.

Remember, busy bee witch, magic is already humming around you, waiting to be embraced. It's the sprinkle of cinnamon on your morning oatmeal, the warmth of the sun on your skin during your commute, and the quiet joy of completing a task. Open your eyes to the magic, and watch your world transform. As you move through your day with a newfound sense of wonder and appreciation, you'll discover that your entire life is a magical practice waiting to be unfolded. This shift in perspective unlocks a world of possibilities. Imagine the grocery aisle as a magical marketplace, filled with ingredients that hold not just flavor but also energetic properties. See your cleaning routine as a ritual of purification, cleansing your space of negativity and creating a sanctuary for positive energy. Even the act of commuting can become a journey of self-discovery, a time to listen to your intuition and set intentions for the day ahead.

This reframing of magic isn't about adding extra tasks to your already overflowing plate. It's about recognizing the magic already present in your life and weaving it into the fabric of your day. By approaching your life with a sense of wonder and intention, you transform the ordinary into the extraordinary. So, grab your metaphorical wand (or your trusty coffee mug!), and get ready to experience the magic that hums within your busy bee life.

Chapter 2: Time Management for the Magically Inclined - Mastering Your Schedule with a Touch of Magic

Ah, time management. It's the ultimate nemesis of the busy bee witch, constantly threatening to drown our magical aspirations in a sea of overflowing inboxes and never-ending to-do lists. But fear not, fellow practitioners! This chapter equips you with powerful tools and a touch of magic to become a master of your schedule, carving out sacred space for your magical practice amidst the daily whirlwind.

Prioritization & The Power of Intention:

The first step to reclaiming your time is prioritizing. Imagine a magical cauldron, overflowing with tasks and obligations. But instead of being a chaotic brew, let's create a potent potion for success. Start by identifying your most important tasks - the ones that absolutely need to be done. These might be your work deadlines, essential errands, childcare responsibilities, or even that doctor's appointment you've been putting off.

Options to Personalize Your Practice:

• **The Career-Focused Witch:** Perhaps your most important tasks involve presentations, reports, or client meetings.

• **The Family-Oriented Witch:** Maybe your top priorities include school pick-ups, grocery shopping for healthy meals, or quality time with loved ones.

• **The Self-Care Witch:** Don't forget to prioritize activities that nourish your mind, body, and spirit. This could be scheduling time for exercise, meditation, or simply getting enough sleep.

Next, consider your magical goals. Do you yearn for a daily morning meditation to center yourself, a moon phase ritual once a month to connect with lunar energies, or simply a few minutes each evening to recharge your magical batteries? Write down these goals and prioritize them alongside your daily tasks.

Now, the magic kicks in! Imbue these priorities with intention. Visualize yourself completing your most important tasks with focus and efficiency. Imagine yourself feeling energized and empowered after your morning meditation or experiencing a sense of peace and connection during your moon phase ritual. When you prioritize with intention, you infuse your schedule with purpose, making it easier to stick to your plan and avoid time-wasting distractions.

Crafting a Realistic & Magical Schedule:

So, you have your priorities, now let's get them on the calendar! Ditch the unrealistic schedules of superhumans. Busy bee witches thrive on practicality. Be honest about how much time you realistically have for each task and magical practice. Think about your energy levels throughout the day. Are you a morning lark or a night owl? Schedule your most demanding tasks when you're at your peak and use quieter moments for your magical practice.

Here's where time blocking comes in - a magical scheduling technique. Block out specific slots in your day dedicated to your most important tasks, including your magical endeavors. Schedule a 10-minute morning meditation, a 30-minute power lunch with a quick visualization for productivity, or an evening bath ritual infused with cleansing herbs before bed. Treat these magical time blocks as sacred appointments, just as important as any work meeting or doctor's visit.

Beyond Time Blocking: Magical Hacks for Busy Bees

But time blocking isn't the only trick up your sleeve! Here are some additional magical hacks to help busy bee witches manage their time like a pro:

- **Batching Similar Tasks:** Group similar errands or chores together to minimize wasted time and mental switching costs. For example, dedicate a specific day to tackling all your bill payments or grocery shopping. This can also be applied to magical practices. If you're working on a spell requiring multiple herbs, gather and prepare them all at once instead of making multiple trips.

- **The Power of "No":** Learning to politely decline requests that drain your time and energy is a crucial magical skill. Remember, protecting your time is essential for protecting your magical practice. politely explain that your schedule is full and offer to reschedule for another time if appropriate.

- **Delegate and Enchant!:** Can't fit everything in? See if there are tasks you can delegate to others. Feeling overwhelmed with laundry? Try a quick laundry-lightening spell while you fold clothes, infusing the task with a little extra magic for a speedier completion. You can also create a charm or sachet to place in your dryer to imbue your clothes with positive energy.

- **Tech Magic to the Rescue!:** Explore apps and digital tools that can help you manage your time more effectively. Utilize calendar apps to block out magical practice time alongside appointments and deadlines. Consider using to-do list apps that allow you to categorize tasks and set reminders to ensure you don't miss a beat.

Quick Tip: Time Management Spells & Visualizations:
Need a little extra oomph in your time management journey? Here are a few quick magical tools to boost your efforts:

- **Time Management Spell:** Light a yellow candle (representing focus) and write down your most pressing tasks on a piece of paper. Visualize yourself completing them efficiently and with ease. Then, burn the paper, releasing your intention into the universe. As the ashes rise, imagine your worries and time constraints dissolving with them.

- **Visualization for Productivity:** Before starting a project, close your eyes and imagine yourself tackling it with laser focus. See yourself completing tasks efficiently and feeling energized throughout the process. Visualize yourself surrounded by a soft, golden light, representing your inner focus and productivity.

Remember, busy bee witch, time management isn't about cramming more into your day, but about strategically prioritizing and scheduling what matters most. By integrating magic into your time management, you'll transform yourself into a master of your schedule and carve out space for both your practical life and your magical practice. Now go forth and conquer that to-do list, all while keeping your magical spark ignited!

Part 2: Magic for Every Moment - Weaving Enchantment into Your Busy Bee Life

The hustle and bustle of daily life doesn't have to extinguish your inner witch! Part 2 dives into the practical magic you can weave throughout your busy bee day. From the energizing morning buzz to the well-deserved evening enchantment, we'll explore simple spells, rituals, and practices to transform each precious moment into a mini magical experience. Get ready to discover how to:

Start your day with intention: Craft a magical morning routine that sets the tone for a productive and fulfilling day.

Options to Personalize Your Practice:

- **The Coffee Connoisseur Witch:** As you grind your coffee beans, infuse them with intention for the day ahead. Visualize success and clarity swirling into the grounds with each rotation. Breathe in the rich aroma, letting it invigorate you and awaken your inner magic.

- **The Meditation Maven Witch:** Perhaps coffee isn't your thing. Begin your day with a short meditation practice. Focus on your breath, centering yourself and setting intentions for the day. If you have a specific goal in mind, visualize yourself achieving it with clarity and ease.

Morning Magic for Everyone:

- **Crystal Clearing:** No matter your morning routine, consider incorporating a quick crystal clearing ritual. Hold your favorite crystal (or a piece of clear quartz) and envision any negativity or sluggish energy dissolving away. Program it with your intentions for the day, like focus, creativity, or positive energy.

- **The Power of Affirmations:** Affirmations are powerful tools for starting your day on the right foot. Repeat positive affirmations to yourself, either silently or aloud, as you get ready. Examples include "I am strong and capable," "I am open to abundance," or "Today is a day of magic and possibility."

Find magic in your lunch break: Transform your midday break into a mini magical retreat for grounding and rejuvenation.
Options for Busy Bee Witches:

- **The Nature Witch:** If you have access to a park or green space, take a mindful walk during your lunch break. Connect with the natural world, focusing on the beauty of a blooming flower or the majestic form of a tree. Feel the grounding energy of the earth beneath your feet as you recharge your spirit.

- **The Meditation Master Witch:** Don't have access to nature? Find a quiet corner and practice a short meditation. Even 5-10 minutes can be enough to center yourself and refocus for the afternoon ahead. Use a guided meditation app if you need help getting started.

Lunchtime Magic for Busy Bees:

- **Gratitude is Magic:** Take a few moments during your lunch break to express gratitude for the good things in your life. Write down three things you're grateful for in a journal, or simply whisper them silently to yourself. This simple act amplifies positive energy and can leave you feeling uplifted and revitalized.

- **The Power of Visualization:** Carve out a few minutes for a quick visualization. Imagine yourself completing your afternoon tasks with efficiency and ease. See yourself radiating positive energy and achieving your goals. Perhaps visualize yourself surrounded by a soft, white light, representing productivity and focus.

Craft a relaxing evening routine: Create a luxurious bath ritual and learn a quick spell to ensure a peaceful night's sleep.

Unwinding Like a Witch:

- **The Bath Ritual Witch:** Transform your bath into a mini magical retreat. Add cleansing herbs like lavender or chamomile to the water, or use essential oils like sandalwood or bergamot for relaxation. Light a few candles and focus on letting go of the day's stress. Visualize tension and negativity draining away as you soak. Let the soothing scent of the herbs or oils fill the room, further enhancing your sense of calm.

- **The Sleepy Spell Witch:** Before lights out, perform a simple sleep spell. Light a calming blue candle (representing peace) and whisper an intention for a restful sleep. You can say something like, "Peaceful dreams I do invite, let worries fade into the night."

Evening Magic for Busy Bees:

- **Moon Magic:** Depending on the moon phase, incorporate its energy into your evening routine. During a waning moon, focus on letting go of anything no longer serving you. Write down any negative thoughts or worries on a piece of paper and then burn it under the moonlight, releasing them symbolically. During a waxing moon, set intentions for what you wish to manifest. Light a white candle (representing new beginnings) and write down your desires in a dedicated journal.

- **Dream Journaling:** Keep a dream journal near your bed and record your dreams upon waking. Dreams can offer valuable insights and guidance. By journaling and reflecting on them, you can unlock their hidden messages and utilize their wisdom in your waking life. Consider spending a few moments before bed meditating on your dreams, allowing intuitive insights to arise.

Busy bee witches, remember: Magic isn't about grand, time-consuming rituals reserved for those with seemingly endless hours. It's about weaving intention and a touch of wonder into the everyday tapestry of your life. By incorporating these simple practices, you'll discover that magic isn't a separate realm, but rather a vibrant thread that runs through every moment. You'll learn to find peace in the quiet hum of your morning commute, feel empowered as you conquer your to-do list, and drift off to sleep with a heart full of gratitude. So, go forth, busy bee witches, and infuse your days with the magic that already exists within you.

Chapter 3: Morning Buzz: Starting Your Day with Intention

The frantic scramble of mornings can leave even the most enthusiastic witch feeling depleted before the day even begins. But what if those precious pre-dawn moments could be transformed into a potent wellspring of magic, setting the tone for a focused and empowered day? Busy bee witches, rejoice! This chapter equips you with simple yet powerful practices to weave magic into your morning routine, ensuring you greet the day with intention and a spark of the extraordinary.

Morning Meditations for Clarity and Focus:

Before the chaos begins, carve out a few precious minutes for a centering meditation. Find a quiet corner, dedicate a few deep breaths to anchoring yourself in the present moment, and gently release any lingering sleepiness. Now, try one of these quick meditations tailored specifically for busy bees:

- **Visualization for Focus (The Early Riser Witch):** If you're an early riser and have a bit more time, consider a visualization practice inspired by nature. Close your eyes and imagine yourself standing on a mountaintop at sunrise. Feel the cool morning air invigorate you as the first rays of sunlight illuminate your path. See yourself radiating confidence and clarity, ready to tackle the day with purpose.

- **Gratitude Meditation for Positive Energy (The Night Owl Witch):** Even if you're short on time, a quick gratitude meditation can be incredibly grounding. As you brush your teeth or make your coffee, silently list three things you're grateful for. It can be something as simple as a good night's sleep, the warmth of the shower, or the excitement for a new day's possibilities. Feel the gratitude wash over you, leaving you feeling positive and energized.

Morning Affirmations: Speaking Your Intentions into Being:
Once grounded in the present, empower yourself with positive affirmations. Speak them with conviction, believing in their power to shape your reality. Here are some examples tailored for the busy bee witch:

- **The Organized Witch:** "I am a master of organization, tackling my tasks with ease and efficiency."

- **The Creative Witch:** "My creative wellspring flows freely today, allowing me to bring innovative solutions to any challenge."

- **The Balanced Witch:** "I find healthy balance between work, personal life, and my magical practice, allowing each to flourish."

Your Simple Morning Altar: A Space for Peace and Power:
Contrary to popular belief, a magical morning altar doesn't require a grand display. Create a simple, sacred space that resonates with you. Dedicate a corner of your nightstand, a shelf on your bathroom mirror, or even a small box tucked away in a drawer. Adorn it with objects that inspire you and enhance your morning routine. Here are some ideas based on your magical focus:

• **The Goal-Oriented Witch:** A small piece of citrine (crystal for abundance and success) and a picture of your current goal.

• **The Grounded Witch:** A smooth river stone and a sprig of rosemary (for remembrance and focus).

• **The Spiritual Witch:** A small statue of a deity you connect with and a feather representing communication with the divine.

Light the candle or incense (if using) as you begin your meditation or affirmations, letting its flame or smoke symbolize your growing focus and intention for the day.

Quick Spell: Blessing Your Coffee (or Tea!) for Focus and Energy:

Ah, the quintessential morning beverage! Before you grab your coffee or tea, take a moment to transform it into a magical potion for focus and energy.

Here are a few options depending on your preference:

• **The Traditional Witch:** Hold your cup with both hands, grounding yourself in the present moment. As you pour your beverage, visualize it filling with vibrant, energizing light. See it coursing through the steam, infusing your drink with positive energy. Stir clockwise three times, symbolically drawing in focus and clarity. Whisper a simple blessing, imbuing your drink with your intention.

• **The Herbal Witch:** Add a pinch of a focus-enhancing herb like rosemary or peppermint to your tea or coffee while visualizing your desired outcome. Stir clockwise and whisper your intention.

- **The Tech-Savvy Witch:** If you're short on time, simply visualize a quick burst of energy flowing from your phone or tablet into your cup as you power it on to check your schedule.

Taking it a Step Further:

Don't underestimate the power of consistency! Integrate these practices into your morning routine and watch the magic compound. You might even find yourself naturally seeking out a few extra minutes each day to deepen your connection with the divine before the day's chaos unfolds. As you become more comfortable with these practices, consider exploring guided meditations specifically designed for focus and productivity. Essential oils can also be powerful allies in your morning routine. Diffuse a blend of invigorating scents like peppermint or rosemary to enhance alertness and focus.

Remember, busy bee witch, even a few stolen moments in the morning can make a world of difference. By incorporating these simple practices, you'll start your day feeling grounded, focused, and empowered to weave magic into the tapestry of your busy life. You'll greet the challenges and opportunities of the day with a sense of calm clarity, ready to manifest your intentions and thrive as a magical being in a bustling world.

Chapter 4: Noon Nirvana: Magical Lunch Break Hacks

The midday slump – a universal experience that can leave even the most energetic witch feeling drained and uninspired. But busy bee witches, fear not! Your lunch break doesn't have to be a wasted hour of scrolling through social media or wolfing down a sad desk lunch. This chapter equips you with magical tools to transform your midday break into a mini-oasis of rejuvenation and inspiration.

Finding Pockets of Magic During Your Lunch Break:

Let's be honest, sometimes a full-blown ritual just isn't feasible during your lunch hour. But that doesn't mean you can't weave magic into your midday break! Here are some ideas to get you started:

- **The Tech Detox Witch:** Give yourself a digital break. Power down your phone and computer, allowing yourself to truly disconnect and recharge. Consider using a "Do Not Disturb" setting or a dedicated app to block distracting notifications.

- **The Mindful Munching Witch:** Turn your lunch into a mini-meditation. Savor each bite, appreciating the colors, textures, and flavors of your food. Focus on the act of chewing and swallowing, allowing your body to fully absorb the nutrients.

- **The Nature Witch:** Even a short walk outside can be a powerful grounding experience. Step into a nearby park or simply observe the world from your office window. Focus on the sights, sounds, and smells of nature, allowing them to wash away any stress or negativity. Research suggests that spending time in nature can lower blood pressure, reduce anxiety, and boost creativity – all essential benefits for a busy bee witch!

Quick Rituals for Busy Bees:

● **The Social Butterfly Witch:** Don't have access to nature? Schedule a quick coffee chat with a positive and inspiring colleague. Positive social interaction can be incredibly energizing and can spark creativity and problem-solving skills.

● **The Music Maven Witch:** Take a few minutes to create a power playlist specifically designed to uplift and energize you. Blast it through your headphones or earbuds and allow the music to wash away stress and refocus your mind for the afternoon.

● **The Bookworm Witch:** Escape into a world of fiction for a mental break. Pack a few chapters of a captivating book and get lost in another world, allowing your mind to relax and recharge.

Going Beyond the Basics: Craft Your Ideal Magical Lunch Break

● **Theme Your Break:** Feeling overwhelmed by paperwork? Pack a picnic lunch and head to a local park for a "Grounding in Nature" break. Facing a creative block? Visit a museum or art gallery for an "Inspiration Infusion" break.

- **Bring Your Magic Tools:** Keep a small pouch or bag with a few magical essentials in your desk drawer. This could include a favorite crystal for grounding, a calming essential oil blend, or a handwritten affirmation card to refocus your intentions.

- **The Power of Visualization:** During your lunch break, take a few minutes to visualize yourself successfully completing your afternoon tasks. See yourself radiating confidence and focus as you tackle your challenges.

Recipe: Creating a Power Lunch Infused with Intention:
Food is more than just fuel; it can be a conduit for magic. Pack a lunch that not only nourishes your body but also supports your magical goals. Here's a simple recipe for a Power Lunch infused with intention:
Ingredients: (Adjust based on your preferences)

- Whole grain bread or salad greens for a base
- Lean protein source like grilled chicken, chickpeas, or tofu
- Colorful vegetables for a variety of vitamins and minerals
- A sprinkle of nuts or seeds for healthy fats and a touch of magic

The Magical Touch:
As you prepare your lunch, infuse it with intention. Visualize the healthy energy flowing into your food, nourishing your body and mind. If you're looking for a specific boost, consider incorporating magical herbs or spices:

- Rosemary for focus and memory
- Turmeric for creativity and vitality
- Spinach for strength and endurance
- Blueberries for protection and mental clarity

- Almonds for wisdom and decision-making

Enjoy with Gratitude:

Savor each bite of your intentionally crafted lunch, appreciating the nourishment it provides for your body and your magical practice. Remember, mindful eating isn't just about physical health; it's about honoring the food that sustains you and thanking the earth for its bounty.

By incorporating these simple hacks and recipes, you can transform your lunch break from a mundane pitstop into a magical oasis. A short walk in nature, a mindful conversation with a friend, or a power lunch filled with intention can all be powerful tools for rejuvenation and inspiration. Remember, busy bee witch, even small pockets of magic woven into your day can make a significant impact on your overall well-being and sense of empowerment. So, step away from your desk, reconnect with yourself and the world around you, and nourish yourself with the magic that awaits you!

Chapter 5: Evening Enchantment: Winding Down After a Busy Day

The day's whirlwind has finally settled, but the lingering buzz of emails and deadlines can make a peaceful night's sleep seem like a distant dream. Busy bee witch, fret no more! This chapter equips you with tools to weave magic into your evening routine, creating a sanctuary for relaxation and rejuvenation. By incorporating these practices, you'll transform those precious pre-sleep moments into an opportunity to cleanse negativity, recharge your batteries, and drift off into a slumber filled with peace and possibility.

Crafting a Relaxing & Magical Evening Routine:

The key to a magical evening routine is intentionality. Just as you carve out space for magic in the morning, dedicate some time before bed to unwind and disconnect from the day's stresses. Here are some ideas to get you started:

- **The Tech Detox Witch:** Set a strict time limit on emails, social media, and work-related tasks. Consider using a blue light filter on your devices in the evening to minimize sleep disruption. Instead, opt for relaxing activities that calm your mind and prepare you for sleep:

  o **The Bookworm Witch:** Curl up with a captivating book in a genre that sparks joy and imagination.

  o **The Music Maestro Witch:** Lose yourself in the soothing melodies of calming music. Create a playlist specifically designed for relaxation and sleep, incorporating binaural beats or nature sounds.

○ **The Bath Bliss Witch:** Take a luxurious bath infused with restorative magic (detailed later in this chapter).

● **The Ambiance Architect Witch:** Dim the lights in your home, creating a calming and sleep-conducive environment. Studies show that exposure to bright lights before bed can disrupt your sleep cycle. Here are some options:

○ **Warm Lighting:** Opt for warm-toned lighting sources like incandescent bulbs or Himalayan salt lamps. Their warm glow promotes relaxation and prepares your body for sleep.

○ **Candlelight Magic:** Light a few candles, infusing the space with a warm and inviting glow that promotes relaxation. Let the flickering candlelight dance on the walls, creating a mesmerizing ambiance that further enhances the magical mood.

● **The Mindful Meditator Witch:** Take a few minutes for mindful breathing or meditation. Focus on your breath, allowing your thoughts to drift away without judgment. If worries persist, write them down on a piece of paper and symbolically release them by burning the paper (safely, of course!). This practice clears your mind of anxieties and helps you achieve a state of inner peace, preparing you for a restful night's sleep.

Bath Ritual: Cleansing Negativity and Embracing Peace:

Transform your evening bath into a magical ritual for cleansing and rejuvenation. Here's how to weave some practical magic into your bath time:

- **Prepare the Space:** Fill your bathtub with warm water and add bath salts or essential oils that promote relaxation, such as lavender, chamomile, or sandalwood. Light candles and play calming music to create a peaceful atmosphere. Let the flickering candlelight dance on the water's surface, creating a mesmerizing ambiance that further enhances the magical mood.

- **Intentional Cleansing:** As you submerge yourself in the warm water, visualize it washing away any lingering negativity or stress from the day. Imagine a cleansing light emanating from within you, dissolving any negativity and leaving your spirit feeling refreshed. Let the soothing warmth of the water seep into your muscles, melting away tension and preparing you for a night of restorative sleep.

- **Nourishing with Herbs:** Consider adding a simple herbal infusion to your bathwater. Herbs like lavender and chamomile are well-known for their calming properties, while rosemary promotes mental clarity and can even aid in lucid dreaming. To create a simple infusion, steep a handful of dried herbs in a cup of hot water for 10 minutes, then strain and add it to your bathwater. Let the herbal essence infuse the water, enveloping you in their restorative properties.

- **Setting Intentions for Sleep:** Before you step out of the bath, take a moment to set your intentions for the night. Close your eyes and visualize yourself falling asleep peacefully, waking up feeling rested and rejuvenated. See yourself waking with renewed energy, ready to embrace a new day filled with magic and possibility. You can even whisper a simple affirmation, such as "Tonight I sleep soundly, waking refreshed and ready to embrace a new day." Speak your intentions with conviction, allowing the power of positive thought to guide you towards a peaceful slumber.

Quick Spell: Creating a Protective Charm for Sweet Dreams:
Sometimes, a simple charm can offer a powerful psychological boost. Here's a quick and easy spell to create a protective charm for sweet dreams:

Gather the Materials:

- A small amethyst crystal (known for promoting peaceful sleep)
- A white piece of string or yarn
- A sprig of lavender (known for its calming properties)

Cleanse and Charge: Cleanse your crystal under running water or by smudging it with sage smoke. Spend a few minutes visualizing it being filled with white light, ready to promote peaceful sleep. Crystals are believed to hold energy, and cleansing them removes any negativity they may have absorbed. By charging the amethyst with white light, you program it with your intention of peaceful sleep.

- **Craft Your Charm:** Tie the amethyst crystal and lavender sprig together using the white string or yarn. Focus on your intention as you tie the knot, visualizing it creating a protective barrier against negativity and promoting peaceful dreams. Whisper a simple incantation, such as "Banish worries, invite rest, sweet dreams upon me be blessed."

• **Place Your Charm:** Hang your charm by your bedside or tuck it under your pillow. As you drift off to sleep, let the amethyst's calming energy and the lavender's soothing scent lull you into a peaceful slumber.

Beyond the Bath: Additional Practices for Restful Sleep

• **The Tea Time Witch:** Enjoy a cup of calming herbal tea before bed. Opt for soothing blends like chamomile, lavender, or valerian root, known for their sleep-promoting properties.

• **The Gratitude Guru Witch:** Take a few minutes before bed to reflect on the things you're grateful for, big or small. Gratitude fosters a sense of peace and well-being, setting the stage for a restful night's sleep.

• **The Dream Weaver Witch:** Keep a dream journal by your bedside. Upon waking, jot down your dreams, even if they seem fragmented. Over time, you may begin to identify recurring themes or symbols, offering insights into your subconscious and potential areas for growth.

Remember, busy bee witch, even a short evening routine infused with magic can make a world of difference. By incorporating these practices, you'll create a sanctuary for relaxation and rejuvenation, allowing you to unwind from the day's stresses and drift off into a sleep filled with peace and the promise of a magical tomorrow. So, light some candles, draw a soothing bath, and let the magic of self-care wash over you. Sweet dreams!

Part 3: Maintaining Your Magical Practice - Busy Bee Style

Life throws a lot our way, busy bees! But amidst the whirlwind, nurturing your magical practice is essential. It's the wellspring of your power and a source of peace and grounding in a chaotic world. Part 3 equips you with tools and strategies to keep your witchcraft flame burning brightly, even with a jam-packed schedule. This section explores ways to:

Embrace the Moon's Magic on the Move:

The moon's ever-changing phases offer a potent source of magical energy. But busy schedules don't have to keep you from harnessing its power. Here are some ways to integrate lunar magic into your life, even on the go:

- **Quick Moon Phase Rituals:** Designate a specific, small action you can take during each moon phase. Here are some ideas:

  ○ **New Moon:** Set intentions for the coming lunar cycle. Write them down in a dedicated moon journal or whisper them under the night sky during your commute home.

  ○ **Waxing Moon:** Focus on growth and manifestation. Carry a moonstone in your pocket as a reminder, or take a few minutes during your lunch break to visualize your goals bathed in moonlight.

○ **Full Moon:** Celebrate culmination and release. Do a quick cleansing ritual by washing your hands with moon water (water charged under the full moon) or spend a few minutes meditating under the moonlight, releasing any negativity you may be holding onto.

○ **Waning Moon:** Focus on letting go and banishing negativity. Write down any unwanted habits or negativity on a piece of paper and symbolically tear it up under the waning moon's light.

● **Moon Phase Tracking Made Easy:** Invest in a pre-made moon phase calendar or create your own! Use a wall calendar or a digital bullet journal app to mark the upcoming moon phases. This allows you to plan your magical activities in advance, ensuring you don't miss a potent lunar window.

Celebrate the Sabbats, Simply:

The eight Wiccan holidays, or Sabbats, mark significant turning points in the earth's seasonal cycle. While elaborate rituals are lovely, they're not always feasible with a busy schedule. Here's how to celebrate the Sabbats in a simple yet meaningful way:

● **Short & Sweet Sabbat Rituals:** Focus on a single, impactful action for each Sabbat. Here are some ideas:

○ **Yule (Winter Solstice):** Light a white candle during your evening meditation, symbolizing the return of light.

○ **Imbolc (Brigid's Day):** Sprinkle a bit of spring flowering water (water infused with spring flowers) on your doorstep, welcoming the coming spring.

○ **Ostara (Spring Equinox):** Plant a seed or sprout indoors, symbolizing new beginnings and growth.

○ **Beltane (May Day):** Leave a small offering of milk and honey for the fairies under a blossoming tree, celebrating fertility and abundance.

○ **Litha (Summer Solstice):** Spend a few minutes basking in the morning sunlight, soaking up its energizing rays.

○ **Lammas (Lughnasad):** Bake a loaf of bread from scratch, celebrating the first harvest.

○ **Mabon (Autumn Equinox):** Take a walk in nature and collect fallen leaves, representing the beauty of transformation and letting go.

○ **Samhain (Halloween):** Light a candle for your ancestors or create a small altar to honor them.

● **Seasonal Altar Magic:** Create a simple, yet beautiful, seasonal altar decoration to enhance your Sabbat rituals. Here are some quick and easy ideas:

○ Use seasonal objects found in nature – pinecones for Yule, blossoming branches for spring Sabbats, seashells for Litha, colorful leaves for Mabon, etc.

○ Decorate a small candle with herbs or spices associated with the Sabbat.

○ Display a piece of artwork or a meaningful quote that embodies the spirit of the Sabbat.

Build Your Busy Bee Coven:

Connection is a vital aspect of witchcraft. A coven, a group of witches working together, can provide support, guidance, and a sense of belonging. But what if you don't have time for regular in-person coven meetings? Here are some ways to build your coven, even with limited time:

- **The Virtual Coven:** Explore online covens that meet via video conferencing or chat forums. This allows you to connect with like-minded individuals from all over the world, even with a busy schedule.

- **The Solitary Spark:** Even as a solitary practitioner, you can still cultivate a sense of connection. Join online witch forums and communities to share experiences, ask questions, and offer support to others.

- **The Local Buzz:** Look for local metaphysical shops or pagan organizations that host workshops or events. Attending even a few times a year allows you to connect with local witches and build a network of support.

Remember, Busy Bee Witches, It's All About Progress, Not Perfection!

Weaving magic into your life doesn't have to be complicated or time-consuming. Even small, intentional actions can make a big difference. Embrace the little moments, celebrate your progress, and don't be discouraged by setbacks. By incorporating the tools and strategies offered in this book, you can maintain a vibrant magical practice that empowers and enriches your life, even amidst the constant buzz. So, busy bee witches, get out there, embrace the magic that surrounds you, and keep your witchy flame burning brightly!

Chapter 6: Moon Magic on the Move: Fitting Lunar Work into Your Busy Life

The moon, our celestial dance partner, has captivated humanity since the dawn of time. Its ever-changing phases hold potent energy, influencing the tides, the growth cycles of plants, and even our emotions. Busy bee witches, rejoice! You can tap into this powerful lunar energy, even amidst your jam-packed schedules. This chapter explores the magic of the moon phases and offers simple rituals and spells that take just minutes to perform, allowing you to integrate moon magic into your already busy life.

The Allure of the Moon Cycles:

The moon goes through a cycle of eight phases, roughly every 28 days. Each phase holds a unique energy, influencing different aspects of our lives. Here's a brief overview:

- **New Moon:** A time for new beginnings, setting intentions, and planting seeds for future growth. It's a powerful time for manifestation as the lunar energy is at its weakest, making space for new beginnings.

- **Waxing Crescent Moon:** A time for initiating projects, boosting energy, and taking action. The moon's energy is building, propelling you forward.

- **First Quarter Moon:** A time for overcoming challenges, facing obstacles head-on, and promoting independence.

This phase is marked by a sense of determination and willpower.

- **Waxing Gibbous Moon:** A time for growth, abundance, and attracting what you desire. The moon's energy is reaching its peak, making it a potent time for spells focused on prosperity and manifestation.

- **Full Moon:** A time for culmination, releasing negativity, and celebrating achievements. The moon's energy is at its fullest, making it a time for culmination, emotional release, and heightened intuition.

- **Waning Gibbous Moon:** A time for reflection, letting go, and banishing unwanted energies. As the moon's energy wanes, it's a natural time for releasing negativity and making space for new beginnings.

- **Third Quarter Moon:** A time for introspection, cleansing, and releasing emotional baggage. This phase is marked by introspection and a need to shed what no longer serves you.

- **Waning Crescent Moon:** A time for rest, divination, and connecting with your intuition. The moon's energy is at its weakest, making it a perfect time for dreamwork and connecting with your inner wisdom.

Quick & Easy Moon Magic for Busy Bees:
Don't let time constraints be a barrier to experiencing the magic of the moon! Here are some simple rituals and spells you can perform for each moon phase, each taking just a few minutes:

- **New Moon:**

○ **Sigil Creation (10 minutes):** A sigil is a personal symbol infused with your intention. During the new moon, design a sigil that represents your desire for the coming lunar cycle. Spend some time focusing on your intention and channeling it into the symbol. You can find many resources online for sigil creation techniques.

○ **Seed Planting Ritual (anytime):** As you plant seeds in your garden or a potted plant, whisper your intentions for growth and abundance into the soil. Visualize the seeds taking root and flourishing under the new moon's influence.

● **Waxing Crescent Moon:**

○ **Sun Salutation Ritual (5 minutes):** Step outside and face the rising sun. Perform a few sun salutations, a common yoga practice, while visualizing the waxing moon's energy filling you with vitality and motivation.

● **First Quarter Moon:**

○ **Obstacle Banishing Spell (3 minutes):** Write down a specific challenge you're facing on a piece of paper. Fold the paper in half and tear it into small pieces, visualizing the obstacle being broken down and overcome with the moon's empowering energy.

● **Waxing Gibbous Moon:**

○ **Abundance Visualization (2 minutes):** Close your eyes and visualize yourself surrounded by symbols of abundance – overflowing baskets, piles of coins, or a flourishing garden. Feel the energy of prosperity flowing into your life with the waxing moon.

- **Full Moon:**

○ **Moon Water Charging (overnight):** Fill a glass jar or bowl with clean water and leave it under the full moon's light overnight. This moon water can be used for cleansing rituals, sprinkling it on your altar or workspace, or even adding a few drops to your bath.

- **Waning Gibbous Moon:**

○ **Negative Energy Release (5 minutes):** Light a black or purple candle (colors associated with cleansing) and write down any negativity you wish to release on a piece of paper. Hold the paper over the flame (safely!) and visualize it burning away, taking your negativity with it.

- **Third Quarter Moon:**

○ **Gratitude Meditation (10 minutes):** Sit comfortably and spend a few minutes focusing on all the things in your life that you're grateful for. Let the feelings of gratitude wash over you, cleansing and renewing your spirit.

- **Banishing Pouch (30 minutes):**

- **Symbolism:** As the moon wanes, use this pouch to release anything negative that no longer serves you.

- **Materials:** Fabric scraps, sewing supplies, herbs associated with banishing (rosemary, mugwort), optional: parchment paper and pen.

- **Instructions:** Sew a small pouch from fabric scraps. While sewing, focus on what you want to let go of. Write your intentions on a piece of parchment paper and place it inside the pouch along with the herbs. Carry the pouch with you as a reminder to release negativity during the waning moon.

Craft Project: Your Personalized Moon Phase Chart:

For busy bee witches like yourself, organization is key! Create a moon phase chart to track the lunar cycle and plan your magical workings. Here's what you'll need:

- A large piece of poster board or cardboard
- Markers, crayons, or paint
- Stickers or small pictures (optional)

*Divide your chart into eight sections, each representing a moon phase. Label each section with the corresponding moon phase name and a symbol. You can find many beautiful moon phase symbols online to use for inspiration.

*Use colors and images to represent the energy of each phase. For example, you could use white for the new moon (new beginnings), yellow for the waxing crescent moon (growth and energy), and so on.

*Once your chart is complete, mark the current moon phase and use it to plan your upcoming rituals and spells. You can also include small pockets or spaces to jot down intentions or notes for each phase.

By creating a personalized moon phase chart, you'll have a beautiful and practical tool to stay connected to the lunar rhythm and easily integrate moon magic into your busy life. Remember, busy bee witch, even a few stolen moments under the moon's glow can weave powerful magic into your everyday existence. So, embrace the ever-changing dance of our celestial companion, and let its light guide you on your magical journey!

Chapter 7: Short and Sweet Sabbat Celebrations

The Wiccan Wheel of the Year marks eight potent Sabbats, each a celebration of a shift in the seasons and holding a unique energy. Busy bee witches, don't despair if elaborate rituals seem out of reach! This chapter explores the importance of these Sabbats and offers pared-down, yet meaningful, ways to celebrate them amidst your busy schedule.

The Enchanting Journey of the Wiccan Wheel of the Year:

The Wiccan Wheel of the Year is a cyclical calendar that tracks the changing seasons and the ever-evolving relationship between the sun and the earth. The eight Sabbats mark the solstices, equinoxes, and cross-quarter days, each imbued with a specific energy that can be harnessed for magical workings and personal growth. Here's a deeper dive into each Sabbat and its essence:

- **Yule (Winter Solstice):** The darkest night of the year, Yule marks the rebirth of the sun and a time for introspection, setting intentions for the coming year, and celebrating new beginnings. It's a perfect time to reflect on what you want to cultivate in the coming cycle. Decorate your altar with evergreen boughs, symbolizing enduring life, and light a white candle, representing the returning light. Consider Yule log traditions or writing down your wishes and burning them (safely!) to symbolize letting go of the old and welcoming the new.

• **Imbolc:** Marking the beginning of spring, Imbolc is a time for purification, honoring ancestors, and celebrating the stirrings of new life after the winter's slumber. It's a time to cleanse your physical and energetic space to make room for new beginnings. Light a white or yellow candle and cleanse your space with smoke from incense or herbs like rosemary or sage. Reflect on the lessons learned during the winter months and prepare for the growth to come. Consider baking a bread called a "bride's cake" to symbolize fertility and new beginnings.

• **Ostara (Spring Equinox):** A time of perfect balance between day and night, Ostara celebrates the arrival of spring, fertility, and new beginnings. The energy is ripe for planting seeds, both literal and metaphorical. Decorate your altar with vibrant flowers and brightly colored candles. Plant seeds outdoors or in a pot, symbolizing your desires and embracing the energy of growth. Create or decorate spring-themed eggs to represent new beginnings and fertility.

• **Beltane:** Falling roughly halfway between spring equinox and summer solstice, Beltane pulsates with the energy of passion, fertility, and life's abundance. It's a time to celebrate life in all its vibrancy. Light a red candle and adorn your altar with brightly colored flowers and greenery. Celebrate Beltane with a bonfire (safely, of course!), symbolizing the sun's fiery energy, or participate in a maypole dance, a traditional expression of fertility and joy. If you have pets, consider weaving a flower crown for them, incorporating herbs associated with protection and well-being.

• **Litha (Summer Solstice):** The longest day of the year, Litha is a time of peak sunlight, celebrating joy, gratitude, and reaching for your goals. Bask in the warmth of the summer sun and savor the long daylight hours. Light a yellow or orange candle and express gratitude for the bounty of the earth. Visualize your most audacious goals coming to fruition. Spend some time outdoors, soaking up the sun's energy and allowing it to charge your own inner fire.

• **Lughnasadh (Lammas):** The first harvest festival, Lughnasadh is a time to celebrate the abundance of the earth, express gratitude for the fruits of your labor, and acknowledge the changing seasons. Decorate your altar with grains, fruits, and vegetables from the harvest. Bake a loaf of bread to honor the earth's bounty and share a meal with loved ones. If you haven't grown anything yourself, visit a farmer's market and select some seasonal produce to express appreciation for the harvest.

• **Mabon (Autumn Equinox):** Marking the second harvest and the return of equal day and night, Mabon is a time of balance, expressing gratitude, and preparing for the approaching darkness. Light an orange or brown candle and adorn your altar with autumnal leaves and gourds. Reflect on the lessons learned throughout the year and practice gratitude for the blessings received. Consider creating a gratitude list or participating in a traditional Mabon dumb supper, where everyone eats in silence to contemplate the year's harvest.

• **Samhain:** The veil between the worlds is thinnest at Samhain, a time to honor the dead, celebrate the ancestors, and reflect on endings and new beginnings. Light an orange or black candle and decorate your altar with offerings for the departed, such as food, flowers, or photographs. Practice ancestral veneration through meditation or journaling, and acknowledge the cyclical nature of life, death, and rebirth. Consider carving a jack-o'-lantern, a tradition with Celtic roots that symbolizes warding off evil spirits and lighting the way for the dead.

Simple Yet Meaningful Sabbat Celebrations for Busy Bees:
Even with a jam-packed schedule, you can still weave the magic of the Sabbats into your life. Here are some ideas for pared-down, yet impactful, Sabbat celebrations that take just a few minutes:

- **Create a Simple Altar:** Dedicate a small corner of your space as a temporary altar. Adorn it with items that resonate with the Sabbat's energy. For Yule, you might include a white candle, evergreen boughs, and cinnamon sticks. For Beltane, incorporate brightly colored flowers, a red candle, and a small maypole decoration (easily crafted from a twig and ribbon).

- **Light a Symbolic Candle:** Take a few minutes to light a candle that reflects the Sabbat's energy. Focus on the flame's warmth and visualize it filling you with the corresponding energy – renewal for Yule, purification for Imbolc, and so on. Journal about your intentions or whisper a simple prayer of gratitude.

- **Seasonal Food Offerings:** Savor a simple meal infused with the season's flavors. For example, enjoy a warm bowl of stew with fresh herbs during Lughnasadh, or indulge in a slice of pumpkin pie with autumn spices during Mabon. As you savor each bite, express gratitude for the earth's bounty and the nourishment it provides.

● **Get Crafty!:** Create a quick, seasonal decoration for your altar. During Ostara, decorate a hard-boiled egg with vibrant patterns to represent new beginnings. For Litha, collect colorful pebbles and arrange them on a small plate to symbolize the sun's warmth. These small acts of creativity connect you to the changing seasons and infuse your space with a touch of Sabbat magic.

Quick Activity: Creating a Seasonal Altar Decoration (continued):

This activity, mentioned earlier, provides a hands-on way to connect with the current season:

● Gather your materials: You'll need a small plate or dish, some colorful dried beans, seeds, or nuts (such as acorns, pine cones, or lentils), and a few sprigs of herbs or dried flowers (depending on the season).

● Create with intention: Arrange the beans, seeds, nuts, and herbs on the plate, letting your intuition guide you. For example, during spring, you might use green lentils and yellow split peas to represent new growth, along with sprigs of rosemary for remembrance and focus. In autumn, use brown lentils and red kidney beans to symbolize the harvest, along with dried orange peels and cinnamon sticks for warmth and abundance.

● Place it on your altar: Let your creation grace your altar throughout the season, serving as a constant reminder of the Sabbat's energy and the ever-turning Wheel of the Year.

Remember, busy bee witch, even small celebrations hold immense power. By incorporating these simple practices, you can weave the magic of the Sabbats into your life, honoring the changing seasons and connecting with the cyclical rhythm of the earth. So, light a candle, create a seasonal offering, and allow yourself to be swept away by the enchanting energy of the Wiccan Wheel of the Year!

Chapter 8: Building Your Busy Bee Coven

The path of a witch, even a busy bee witch, is rarely a solitary journey. The power of community, of sharing experiences, and drawing strength from a coven can be invaluable. A coven, a group of witches working together, provides a safe space for shared knowledge, support, and accountability. In a coven, you can learn from more experienced practitioners, celebrate milestones together, and draw strength from the collective energy of your fellow witches.

But busy schedules and geographical distances can make traditional coven meetings a challenge. Fear not, fellow witch! This chapter explores the magic of building your coven, even amidst the whirlwind of daily life.

The Allure of the Coven: Why Community Matters

Witchcraft is a practice steeped in tradition and connection. Covens have existed for centuries, offering a safe space for witches to learn, grow, and celebrate their shared beliefs. Here are just a few reasons why coven life can be so enriching:

- **Shared Knowledge and Diverse Perspectives:** Covens bring together witches with varying levels of experience and expertise. This creates a rich learning environment where you can glean valuable knowledge from seasoned practitioners and offer your own insights to those who are newer to the path. Imagine learning herbal lore from a wise elder witch or sharing your tech-savvy approach to creating magical sigils with the coven!

- **Accountability and Support:** Walking the path of witchcraft can be challenging at times. A coven provides a supportive network where you can share your struggles, celebrate your successes, and receive encouragement from those who understand your unique journey. Perhaps you're facing a difficult decision or simply feeling uninspired magically. Your coven sisters can offer a listening ear, advice based on their experiences, and a reassuring presence to help you navigate the challenges.

- **Collective Energy and Ritual Amplification:** There's a power in numbers. When witches come together in ritual, their combined energy can create a potent magical force, amplifying the effectiveness of spells and workings. Imagine the energy swirling as you raise a full moon circle with your coven, each member contributing their intention and focus to create a powerful magical current.

- **Friendship and Camaraderie:** Beyond the magical aspects, covens offer a sense of belonging and acceptance. You'll forge deep friendships with like-minded individuals who share your passion for witchcraft and can celebrate the joys and challenges of life together. Your coven sisters become your chosen family, a source of laughter, support, and shared experiences that go beyond the magical realm.

Busy Bees and the Coven Conundrum:

The desire for connection might be strong, but let's face it, busy bee witches often have jam-packed schedules and limited free time. Coordinating regular in-person coven meetings can feel like an impossible feat. But fret not! Here are some creative ways to build your coven and connect with your magical community, even amidst a busy life:

The Virtual Coven: Connecting Through Technology:

The digital age offers a wealth of opportunities for witches on the go. Explore the possibility of a virtual coven! Here's how it can work:

- **Online Platforms:** Utilize video conferencing platforms like Zoom or Google Meet to hold regular coven meetings. This allows you to connect with fellow witches from all over the world, regardless of location. Imagine holding an esbat ritual under the full moon with witches from different time zones, each contributing their unique energy to the shared experience.

- **Online Forums and Communities:** Many online forums and social media groups cater specifically to witches. These platforms offer a space for discussions, sharing resources, and fostering a sense of community, even if interactions are primarily virtual. [Online Resource: Finding online witch forums and communities] Perhaps you can find a forum dedicated to a specific tradition of witchcraft that interests you, or a local Facebook group for witches in your area, even if you don't necessarily meet in person.

- **Collaborative Projects:** Work on magical projects together virtually. Perhaps you can choose a specific moon phase or upcoming Sabbat and each member can contribute a ritual or spell to be shared with the group. This fosters a sense of connection and allows you to learn from each other's practices. Imagine collaborating on a virtual Book of Shadows, with each member contributing their favorite spells, recipes, and magical knowledge.

The Solo Witch with a Social Heart:

Maybe a coven, virtual or otherwise, doesn't quite fit your lifestyle. But that doesn't mean you have to go it alone! Here are some ways to cultivate a sense of connection for the solitary practitioner:

- **Find a Magical Pen Pal:** Connect with another solitary witch through email or snail mail. Share your experiences, magical workings, and offer each other support on your individual paths. Imagine building a deep friendship with another witch who understands your solitary practice, exchanging letters filled with magical insights and personal updates.

- **Online Courses and Workshops:** Many online platforms offer witchcraft courses and workshops. These can be a fantastic way to learn new skills, connect with other witches (even if virtually), and feel a sense of belonging to a larger magical community. Imagine enrolling in an online herbalism course and interacting with other witches who share your interest in the magical properties of plants.

- **Engage with Online Resources:** The internet is overflowing with valuable resources for witches. Subscribe to blogs written by witches you admire, follow them on social media, and participate in online discussions to stay connected with the wider magical world. Imagine following a blog that delves into moon magic, learning new rituals and practices each month to incorporate into your solitary work.

- **Local Metaphysical Shops:** Check to see if there are any metaphysical shops in your area. These shops often host workshops, classes, and events that can be a great way to connect with other local witches, even if you don't necessarily form a coven. Imagine attending a crystal healing workshop at a local metaphysical shop, meeting other witches interested in the energetic properties of crystals.

Building Your Busy Bee Coven – It's All About Connection:

Remember, busy bee witch, a coven, virtual or otherwise, should enhance your practice, not add to your stress. The key is to find a way to connect with others who share your passion for witchcraft, even if your interactions are limited by your busy schedule. Don't be afraid to experiment, find what works best for you, and build a coven structure that complements your lifestyle and allows you to tap into the magic of community.

Online Resource: Finding Online Witch Forums and Communities:

The internet offers a vast landscape for witches to connect. Here are some resources to get you started, but remember this is just a starting point. Be sure to explore and find communities that resonate with you!

- **Websites:**

  ○ WitchesOfTheCraft.com

  ○ Llewellyn.com (This website also offers a wealth of educational resources on witchcraft)

  ○ PaganSpace.net (A website specifically dedicated to Pagan and Wiccan communities)

- **Social Media Groups:** Many social media platforms have groups dedicated to witchcraft. Search for terms like "Witches," "Paganism," or "Green Witch" to find relevant groups in your area or with specific interests.

Remember, busy bee witch, you don't have to walk your path alone. By embracing the power of community, even virtually, you can tap into a network of support, share your experiences, and weave a richer tapestry of magic into your life. So, put yourself out there, explore the possibilities, and find your coven, however it may take shape.

Part 4: Expanding the Magical Toolkit - Busy Bee Edition

Your magical journey doesn't have to be confined by the walls of your home or the limitations of a traditional schedule! Part 4 explores innovative ways to expand your witchcraft practice beyond the basics. We'll delve into techniques for incorporating magic into the most unexpected aspects of your busy bee life, from transforming mundane tasks into mini-rituals to harnessing the power of technology for a digital grimoire. Discover how to:

Weave Spells into Your Everyday:

- **Magical Cleaning:** Transform cleaning from a chore into a magical act of purification. Light a cleansing incense like sage or lemongrass as you work, infusing your space with positive energy. While dusting, visualize negative energy and stagnant vibes being swept away. As you mop the floor, imagine cleansing negativity and creating a fresh foundation for new beginnings. You can even play uplifting music that sets the mood for your magical cleaning ritual.

- **Commuter's Commute:** Long commutes can be a great opportunity for magical practice. Listen to guided meditations or podcasts on witchcraft topics. Use your travel time for visualization exercises. Perhaps visualize yourself achieving a goal or attracting your desired outcome. If you take public transportation, carry a charm bag filled with herbs or crystals corresponding to your intention for the day. Consider creating a playlist filled with calming or energizing music, depending on your needs for the day, to further enhance your magical commute.

- **Shopping with Intention:** Grocery shopping can be infused with magic! Plan your meals with the intention of nourishing your body and spirit. As you select fruits and vegetables, focus on their vibrant colors and visualize them infusing you with vitality. When choosing herbs and spices, consider their magical properties and incorporate them into your meals for an added energetic boost. You can even create a shopping list categorized by intention. For instance, if you're looking to boost your creativity, you might list rosemary, known for its memory-enhancing properties, or basil, associated with inspiration.

Embrace Tech Magic:

- **Digital Grimoire:** In our tech-driven world, the traditional grimoire can be reborn in the digital age. There are many apps designed for witches, allowing you to record spells, rituals, and magical observations. You can also use note-taking apps like Evernote or OneNote to create your own digital grimoire, complete with images, videos, and even audio recordings of chants or spells. Explore options for organizing your digital grimoire by topic, moon phase, or even color-coding your entries for easy reference.

- **Magical Apps:** Explore the vast array of apps designed to enhance your practice. Find moon phase trackers to stay informed about lunar cycles and their magical influences. Utilize meditation apps to deepen your focus and relaxation during magical workings. Experiment with apps that create virtual spell jars, allowing you to combine digital elements that resonate with your intention. There are even apps for dream interpretation, helping you decipher the symbolic messages your subconscious might be sending you.

• **Online Resources:** The internet is overflowing with valuable resources for witches. Subscribe to blogs and YouTube channels run by experienced practitioners. Join online forums and communities to connect with other witches, ask questions, and share experiences. The digital world offers a wealth of knowledge and inspiration to expand your magical toolkit. Consider following social media accounts dedicated to specific areas of witchcraft that interest you, such as herbal magic or crystal healing, to deepen your knowledge in those areas.

Travel with Your Practice:

• **Portable Altar:** Create a travel altar that allows you to maintain your practice even when you're on the go. A small box or pouch can hold essential items like crystals, herbs, tarot cards, or miniature statues of deities. You can even create a travel altar using a beautiful scarf or piece of fabric, placing your chosen magical items upon it for rituals. If you're flying, be sure to research travel restrictions for any items you plan to bring in your carry-on luggage.

• **Travel-Friendly Rituals:** Certain rituals can be easily adapted for travel. Perform a shortened version of your morning or evening practice in your hotel room. Spend time meditating in nature, focusing on the sights, sounds, and smells of your new environment. Collect natural elements like pinecones, feathers, or smooth stones as magical mementos of your journey. You can even cleanse your travel altar with a visualization technique, imagining white light enveloping your altar items and infusing them with positive energy.

● **Tech-Aided Travel Magic:** There are many ways to utilize technology to enhance your travel magic. Use a compass app to find the cardinal directions for creating a sacred space during your travels. Download e-books on Wiccan traditions or pagan rituals to continue your magical studies on the go. There are even apps with guided visualizations specifically designed for travel, allowing you to connect with the energy of a new place. Consider using a language translation app to learn basic greetings or phrases in the local language, a small act of respect that can also feel magically connective to the land and its people.

● Remember, busy bee witch, technology is your friend! Embrace the vast array of digital tools and resources at your disposal to weave magic into the fabric of your everyday life. From transforming chores into mini-rituals to creating a digital grimoire, let your tech-savvy shine and expand your magical toolkit in innovative and practical ways. So, pack your metaphorical (and literal) bags, embrace the magic of the journey, and weave your witchcraft into every aspect of your busy bee life.

Chapter 9: Everyday Magic: Weaving Spells into Your Day

Busy bee witches, listen up! Magic isn't confined to elaborate rituals or moonlit ceremonies. The essence of witchcraft lies in infusing intention and awareness into everyday activities. This chapter explores the art of weaving simple spells and visualizations into your daily routine, transforming even the most mundane tasks into opportunities for magical empowerment.

Mundane to Marvelous: Transforming Your Day with Everyday Magic

Our days are filled with a whirlwind of tasks – cleaning, commuting, grocery shopping, the list goes on. But what if we told you these seemingly ordinary activities could be infused with magic? By incorporating intention and a touch of witchery, you can transform your daily routine into a series of mini-rituals, empowering yourself and enriching your experience.

Here are some ways to weave magic into your everyday life:

Mindful Cleaning: Transform your cleaning routine from a chore to a magical practice. Visualize dust and dirt being banished as you clean, representing the purging of negativity from your space. Play uplifting music and infuse your cleaning products with essential oils like lavender for purification or lemon for cleansing energy. Light a white candle while you clean, further symbolizing the banishment of negativity and the restoration of order. As you move through your space, you can even chant a simple mantra under your breath, like "Clean and clear, negativity disappears."

Commuter's Calm: Commuting can be a stressful experience. But it doesn't have to be! Use your commute as a time for mindfulness and meditation. Practice deep breathing exercises or recite a calming mantra to ease any anxieties. Visualize yourself arriving at your destination feeling refreshed and focused. Perhaps you imagine yourself surrounded by a white light, a protective bubble shielding you from the external chaos of traffic or crowded trains. If you take public transportation, use the time to delve into a captivating book or podcast on a topic that inspires you. This will not only elevate your mood but can also spark new ideas and fuel your creativity.

Magical Meal Prep: Grocery shopping and meal prep can be infused with magic as well! Choose your ingredients with intention, selecting fruits and vegetables that correspond to your magical goals. For example, opt for leafy greens for abundance, oranges for vitality, or apples for knowledge. As you cook, visualize your meals nourishing your body and fueling your magical endeavors. Infuse your kitchen with positive affirmations or chants as you prepare your meals, further programming your food with your intentions. For an extra touch of magic, you can write a sigil (a symbol imbued with your intention) on a bay leaf and add it to your dish while it simmers.

Quick Spell: Enchantment for a Productive Cleaning Session

Feeling overwhelmed by a messy space? This quick spell can help you tackle your cleaning session with renewed energy and a touch of magic!

Gather the Supplies:

- You'll need a small bowl of water,
- a pinch of salt (for purification), and
- a sprig of rosemary (for cleansing and focus).

If you have any cleansing incense, like sage or lavender, light it to further purify the space as you clean.

Cast the Spell:

1. Sprinkle the salt into the water and hold the rosemary sprig.
2. Visualize the water absorbing any negativity or clutter energy from your space.
3. Dip the rosemary sprig into the water and flick it around the room, focusing on areas that need the most attention.
4. Chant a simple mantra, such as "Cleanse this space, banish clutter's hold, make cleaning swift, a story to be told."

Get Cleaning!

With renewed energy and a clear intention, begin your cleaning session. Remember, you've just cast a magical spell to empower your efforts! Play some upbeat music to keep your energy high, and take breaks as needed to avoid burnout. Cleaning can be a form of exercise, so embrace the movement and feel the satisfaction of transforming your space.

Quick Visualization: Commuter's Visualization for a Peaceful Journey

Stuck in traffic or facing a long commute? This calming visualization can help you navigate your journey with peace and focus.

Find a Quiet Moment:

1. Close your eyes and take a few deep breaths.
2. Visualize yourself surrounded by a white light, a bubble of peace protecting you from the external chaos.

See Your Destination:

1. Imagine yourself arriving at your destination feeling refreshed and focused. See yourself calmly navigating the traffic or stepping off the train feeling energized and ready for the day ahead.

Embrace the Journey:

1. Focus on your breath and acknowledge the present moment. Accept that delays or crowded commutes are simply part of the journey, and allow yourself to remain calm and centered amidst the external noise.

2. You can also use this time for positive affirmations. Silently repeat mantras that promote patience, focus, or gratitude, depending on what you need most during your commute. If you find your mind wandering to worries, gently guide your focus back to your breath and the visualization of your peaceful arrival.

Beyond the Basics: Everyday Magic for Every Need

The possibilities for incorporating everyday magic are endless! Here are some additional ideas to inspire you:

- **Morning Motivation:** Start your day with a positive intention. Write down an affirmation or goal in your journal, and visualize yourself achieving it throughout the day.

- **Power Shower:** Transform your shower into a mini-ritual for cleansing and rejuvenation. Infuse your shower steam with essential oils like peppermint for energy or eucalyptus for clarity. Visualize negativity washing away with the water as you cleanse your body.

- **Tech Magic:** Embrace technology as a tool for your magic! Use apps to track moon phases, find guided meditations, or create digital sigils to represent your intentions. There are even apps for dream interpretation, helping you decipher the messages your subconscious might be sending you.

- **Nature's Magic:** Take a mindful walk in nature and connect with the earth's energy. Ground yourself by feeling the soil beneath your feet and breathe in the fresh air. Notice the sights, sounds, and smells of nature, appreciating the beauty and power of the world around you.

Remember, busy bee witch, even the most mundane tasks hold the potential for magic. By weaving intention and simple practices into your daily routine, you can transform your ordinary day into an extraordinary experience. Infuse your actions with awareness, turning them into mini-rituals that empower you and enrich the tapestry of your magical life.

Chapter 10: Tech Magic: Your Digital Grimoire

Busy bee witches, rejoice! In our ever-evolving digital world, technology can be a powerful tool for enhancing your witchcraft practice. This chapter explores the concept of "Tech Magic," showcasing how smartphones, tablets, and computers can be utilized to create digital altars, track lunar cycles, and even craft digital spell jars.

Weaving Tech into the Fabric of Your Craft

Remember the days of bulky grimoires and cumbersome tools? Technology offers a modern witch a plethora of resources and tools to streamline your practice and keep it accessible, even amidst your busy schedule. Here are some ways to embrace Tech Magic and weave it into the fabric of your witchcraft:

The Digital Altar: Gone are the days of needing a dedicated physical space for your altar. With a little creativity, you can create a beautiful and functional digital altar on your phone, tablet, or computer. Here's how to get started:

- **Finding Your Focus:** Consider your current magical focus. Are you working on a new moon ritual for attracting abundance? Perhaps you're seeking clarity and focus during a waning moon phase. Choose a digital wallpaper image that resonates with your intention. This could be a moon phase graphic depicting the current lunar cycle, a nature scene that evokes feelings of peace and tranquility during workings focused on inner peace, or an image of a specific deity you revere.

● **Digital Tools:** Collect digital images of crystals, herbs, candles, or other magical tools you would typically use on a physical altar. There are many websites that offer free, high-quality images for download. You can also take photos of your own physical tools and incorporate them into your digital altar.

● **Arranging Your Space:** Arrange your chosen digital elements on your altar screen. Group them aesthetically and intuitively, or position them according to the cardinal directions (north, south, east, west) if that resonates with your practice. Swap out the elements on your digital altar as needed to reflect your current intentions. For instance, during a new moon focused on new beginnings, you might incorporate imagery of a white candle, amethyst crystals (known for their protective qualities), and a moonstone (associated with intuition and fresh starts).

Magical Apps at Your Fingertips: The world of mobile apps offers a treasure trove of resources for busy bee witches, and witches of all backgrounds for that matter. Here are just a few examples to get you started, but don't be afraid to explore and find apps that resonate with your unique practice:

● **Moon Phase Trackers:** Stay connected to the lunar rhythm, a core aspect of witchcraft, with apps that display the current moon phase, upcoming astrological events, and even offer information on moon magic rituals tailored to the specific lunar energy. These can be invaluable tools for aligning your magical workings with the celestial cycles.

Look for features like customizable notifications to remind you of important moon phases or upcoming rituals.

• **Meditation Apps:** Busy schedules often leave us feeling stressed and disconnected from our inner selves. Meditation apps offer guided meditations on a variety of topics, promoting relaxation, focus, and inner peace – all essential ingredients for a successful magical practice. Whether you seek meditations to enhance your visualization during spellwork or simply to unwind after a long day, there's a meditation app out there to suit your needs. Some apps even offer meditations specifically designed for witches, incorporating elements of Wiccan or Pagan practices.

• **Digital Spell Jars:** Love the concept of spell jars, those charming vessels filled with magical ingredients to manifest your desires, but short on time or physical supplies? There are apps that allow you to create digital spell jars. Here's how they work: Choose your intention, select virtual representations of herbs, crystals, and other magical elements from the app's library (or upload your own images if available), and shake your digital jar to infuse it with your energy. These digital spell jars can be just as potent as their physical counterparts, offering a convenient and portable way to carry your magic with you wherever you go. Some apps allow you to set reminders associated with your digital spell jar, prompting you to revisit your intention and refocus your energy throughout the day.

Beyond Busy Bee – Tech Magic for All Witches
Tech Magic isn't just for busy bees! Witches of all walks of life can benefit from the convenience and accessibility that technology offers.

Here are some additional ways to embrace Tech Magic and integrate it into your practice:

- **Digital Grimoire:** Ditch the bulky notebooks and overflowing binders, and create a digital grimoire on your computer or tablet. Use note-taking apps like Evernote, OneNote, or even Google Docs to document your spells, rituals, magical experiences, and anything else you deem important for your practice. This allows for easy organization with searchable tags or categories. You can also add photos, videos, or even audio recordings of chants or spells to enrich your digital grimoire. Consider using a cloud-based storage system to ensure your digital grimoire is backed up and accessible from any device.

- **Online Witchcraft Communities:** The internet connects you to a vast network of fellow witches, offering a sense of community and belonging that can be especially valuable for solitary practitioners. Explore online forums, social media groups, and websites dedicated to witchcraft. Here are some ways to get involved:

  ○ **Engage in Discussions:** Ask questions, share your experiences, and learn from others who share your passion for the craft. Look for groups or forums that align with your specific interests within witchcraft, such as herbal magic, crystal healing, or a particular tradition like Wicca or Paganism.

  ○ **Share Experiences:** Post pictures of your altar, digital spell jars, or any other creative ways you've incorporated Tech Magic into your practice.

○ **Build Connections:** Many online communities allow you to connect with other witches on a more personal level. You might find a coven online or simply develop meaningful friendships with like-minded individuals who can support you on your magical journey. Remember the resources listed in Chapter 8: Building Your Busy Bee Coven can also be applied to finding online communities.

● **Educational Resources:** The internet is brimming with educational resources on witchcraft, making it easier than ever to deepen your knowledge and understanding of the craft. Here are some ways to learn and grow online:

○ **Websites and Blogs:** Find websites and blogs written by reputable witches. Look for content creators who resonate with your interests and approach to witchcraft.

○ **Online Courses:** Take online courses taught by experienced practitioners. There are courses available on a wide range of witchcraft topics, from herbalism and astrology to spellcasting and creating your own rituals.

○ **Videos:** Watch informative videos on various witchcraft topics on platforms like YouTube. There are many witches who share their knowledge and practices through video tutorials and discussions.

● **Embrace the Digital Age:** Don't be afraid to experiment and find ways to integrate technology seamlessly into your witchcraft practice. Technology can be a powerful tool for organization, learning, and staying connected to your magical community. Here are some additional ideas to get you started:

○ **Digital Divination Tools:** There are apps that allow you to perform digital versions of traditional divination practices, such as rune casting or tarot readings. While these may not hold the same weight for everyone as physical tools, they can be a convenient way to gain insights or guidance when you don't have access to physical tools.

○ **Finding Inspiration:** Use Pinterest or Instagram to create vision boards or mood boards that embody your magical goals. Look for images of rituals, spells, herbs, crystals, or anything else that inspires you.

○ **Music Streaming Services:** Create playlists specifically for your magical workings. Uplifting music can enhance positive energy during spells, while calming music can promote relaxation and focus during meditation or divination.

By embracing Tech Magic, busy bee witches (and witches of all stripes!), you can weave a vibrant and accessible magical practice into the fabric of your modern life. Remember, there's no one-size-fits-all approach to witchcraft. Find what technological tools resonate with you and use them to amplify your intentions, streamline your practice, and connect with the ever-evolving world of magic in the digital age.

Chapter 11: Busy Bee Travel Magic: Taking Your Practice on the Go

Busy bee witches, wanderlust can strike at any time! But what about your witchcraft practice when travel beckons? Fear not! This chapter equips you with tips and tricks for maintaining your magical connection, even amidst the hustle and bustle of exploring new destinations.

Hitting the Road (or the Skies) Without Leaving Your Magic Behind

Traveling offers a chance to broaden your horizons, experience new cultures, and create lasting memories. However, busy bee witches often worry about their practice falling by the wayside during adventures. Here are some tips to ensure your witchcraft travels with you:

Planning is Key:

Before embarking on your journey, consider the limitations you might face. Researching your destination is key! Here are some things to consider:

- **Accommodation:** Are you staying in a hotel with limited space, or will you have access to a private outdoor area for rituals? Look for rentals with balconies or patios if possible, especially if fire safety is a concern regarding burning candles or incense.

- **Local Supplies:** Research your destination to see if there are any metaphysical shops you can visit for supplies if needed. This way, you can pack light and replenish essential oils, herbs, or crystals during your travels.

● **Packing Essentials:** Pack a small travel altar kit (more on that coming up!) and any essential oils or crystals you use regularly in your practice. Consider the size and weight restrictions of your luggage, especially if you're flying. Small, polished crystals are easier to pack than large, raw ones. Opt for essential oils in rollerball vials for easy application and to avoid the risk of spills.

Adapt and Improvise:

Sometimes, elaborate rituals just aren't feasible while traveling. Embrace the concept of adaptable witchcraft! Here are some ideas:

● **Shortened Rituals:** Perhaps you can perform shortened versions of your usual rituals or find creative ways to substitute ingredients you can't bring with you. For instance, if your morning ritual involves lighting a white candle and burning incense for purification, you can substitute the candle with visualization – picturing a white light enveloping you and cleansing your energy. For incense, carry a small vial of calming essential oil like lavender and dab a drop on your wrists or temples.

● **Tech Substitutions:** There are many digital resources available for witches on the go. Consider using meditation apps for guided meditations in place of your usual practice, or listening to nature sounds to connect with the local elements if you can't perform a ritual outdoors.

● **Travel-Friendly Ingredients:** Some herbs can be easily packed and used in travel rituals. For example, mugwort tea is a great sleep aid and can be easily brewed in a hotel room with a hot water kettle. Rosemary is another option - a sprig can be tucked into your luggage and used for purification by burning it (following fire safety guidelines!) or by steeping it in hot water for a cleansing bath.

Embrace the Local Magic:

Traveling is a fantastic opportunity to immerse yourself in the local culture and explore its unique magical traditions. Here are some ways to integrate local magic into your travels:

- **Visit Sacred Sites:** Explore temples, sacred sites, or historical landmarks that resonate with your practice. Many cultures have designated places of power that hold a special energy. Visiting these locations can be a deeply moving and spiritually enriching experience.

- **Discover Local Traditions:** Learn about the folklore, myths, and legends of the places you visit. Are there any local deities or spirits that resonate with you? Can you incorporate them into your travel meditations or visualizations?

- **Explore Local Practices:** If appropriate, attend local religious ceremonies or festivals. Immerse yourself in the sights, sounds, and smells of these rituals, taking note of any elements that resonate with your own practice. Be respectful of local customs and traditions, and only participate if you feel welcome.

- **Shop Local Magic:** Visit metaphysical shops or markets to find herbs, crystals, or other magical tools native to the region. These can serve as beautiful mementos of your travels and add a touch of local flair to your practice back home.

The Portable Altar: Your Magical Companion on the Go
A portable altar is a lifesaver for the traveling witch. Here are some ideas to create your own:

- **The Boxy Witch:** Repurpose a small decorative box or jewelry case as your travel altar. Line it with soft fabric and include miniature representations of your typical altar tools – a tiny white candle (battery-operated tea lights are perfect for travel!), a set of travel-sized herb vials, and smooth stones or crystals that fit comfortably inside. Print out small images of tarot cards or sigils that resonate with you and add them to your box for a touch of personalization. This way, you have a complete mini-altar that can be tucked away in your luggage.

- **The Bookworm Witch:** If you're tight on space, consider a travel-sized notebook as your portable altar. Decorate the cover with sigils or magical symbols and use the pages to write down your spells, intentions, or reflections during your travels. You can even include small pressed flowers or leaves collected during your journey, imbuing your grimoire with the essence of your travels. This creates a personalized and portable record of your magical experiences on the road.

- **The Digital Witch:** Embrace Tech Magic! Create a digital altar on your phone or tablet (as discussed in Chapter 10: Tech Magic: Your Digital Grimoire). This allows for ultimate portability and lets you customize it with images and symbols that resonate with the specific location you're visiting. Perhaps you can find pictures of the local deities, landmarks, or natural wonders that inspire you and incorporate them into your digital altar for a truly immersive experience.

Travel-Friendly Rituals and Spells:

Busy bee witches on the go can still perform meaningful rituals and spells, even with limited time and resources. Here are some ideas:

- **Gratitude Ritual:** Take a few moments each day to express gratitude for your travels. Find a quiet spot in your hotel room, a park bench, or even a bustling marketplace, light a small candle (battery-operated tea lights are perfect for travel!), and focus on the blessings you're experiencing. Thank the universe for the opportunity to explore new places, meet new people, and broaden your horizons.

- **Stargazing Spell:** Under the vast expanse of a foreign sky, connect with the celestial realm. Find a secluded spot away from city lights, lay down a blanket or towel, and gaze at the stars. Identify constellations you might not see at home and whisper a wish or intention to the universe. Let the vastness of the cosmos inspire you and remind you of the interconnectedness of all things.

- **Elemental Offering:** As you travel, take a moment to connect with the local elements. Find a beautiful seashell by the ocean and offer it back to the water as a token of gratitude. Leave a small piece of fruit or bread at the base of a majestic tree in a park. Light a small incense stick (be mindful of fire restrictions!) and let the smoke carry your intentions on the wind. These simple offerings acknowledge the land you're visiting and connect you with the elemental forces that shape our world.

Remember, Busy Bee Witches, Travel is Magic!

Travel is an opportunity to expand your magical practice and connect with the world in new and exciting ways. Embrace the spirit of adventure, find creative ways to maintain your practice on the go, and weave magic into the very fabric of your travels.

Part 5: Deepening the Connection with Nature - A Busy Bee's Guide

The natural world is a powerful source of magic, and even busy bees can benefit from its grounding energy and endless inspiration. Part 5 explores ways to cultivate a deeper connection with nature, even amidst a packed schedule. We'll delve into practical techniques for incorporating the magic of plants and the natural world into your busy bee lifestyle. Discover how to:

Embrace Busy Bee Gardening Magic:

- **The Potted Paradise:** Limited on space? No problem! Create a container herb garden on your windowsill, balcony, or fire escape. Choose herbs with short growing seasons and minimal maintenance needs, such as basil, mint, rosemary, or thyme. Not only will you have fresh ingredients readily available for spells and rituals, but tending to your little herb haven can be a calming and grounding experience.

- **The Speedy Seedling:** Short on time but yearning for a more extensive garden? Opt for fast-growing herbs like cilantro, dill, or arugula. These can be started from seed indoors just a few weeks before the last frost and transplanted outdoors for a quick harvest.

- **Magical Meal Prep:** Infuse your meals with a touch of magic! Plant a small kitchen garden with vegetables like peppers, tomatoes, or leafy greens. As you cook with these homegrown ingredients, visualize their vibrant energy nourishing your body and spirit.

● **The Spellcasting Herb Patch:** Research herbs traditionally used in witchcraft and plant a selection that resonates with your practice. Lavender for calming, rosemary for purification, or chamomile for peace are all easy-to-grow options that can be incorporated into a variety of spells and rituals.

Quick Spells and Easy Rituals with Readily Available Plants: Even a busy bee can weave nature's magic into their practice with short, impactful rituals. Here are some ideas:

● **Morning Sun Salutation:** As the first rays of sunlight peek through your window, stand tall with your arms outstretched towards the sun. Visualize the sun's warmth infusing you with energy and focus for the day ahead. Whisper a word of thanks to the sun for its life-giving power.

● **Moonlit Meditation:** Under the glow of the full moon, find a quiet spot outdoors or by a window. Close your eyes, take deep breaths, and allow the moon's light to bathe you in its silvery essence. Focus on releasing negativity and anxieties, letting them drift away on the moonbeams.

● **Gratitude Walk:** During your midday break, take a brisk walk in a nearby park or green space. Pay attention to the sights, sounds, and smells of nature. Notice the vibrant colors of flowers, the rustling of leaves in the breeze, and the chirping of birds. Silently express gratitude for the beauty and peace that nature offers.

- **Herbal Infusions:** Steep readily available herbs like chamomile or lavender in hot water to create a calming tea. As you sip the tea, focus your intention on relaxation or stress relief. Visualize the calming properties of the herbs soothing your mind and body.

- **Sigil Creation with Nature:** Find a fallen leaf, smooth rock, or piece of driftwood on your nature walk. Cleanse it with running water or sunlight. As you hold the natural object, visualize your intention for a spell or ritual. Carve or draw a sigil (a symbol representing your intention) into the object. Carry it with you as a reminder of your focused intention.

Find Magic in Every Moment:

Busy bee witches can cultivate a connection with nature by incorporating short bursts of mindfulness into their daily routine. Here are some ways to find magic in the everyday:

- **Cloud Gazing:** Take a few minutes during your lunch break to lie down on a grassy patch and gaze at the clouds. See whimsical shapes and formations. Let your imagination soar and connect with the vastness of the sky.

- **Mindful Commute:** If you commute by bus or train, use the travel time to connect with nature. Look out the window and appreciate the trees, buildings, and landscapes you pass. Notice the changing colors of the sky throughout the day.

- **Barefoot Connection:** When safe and appropriate, remove your shoes and walk on grass, dirt, or sand. Feel the earth beneath your feet and reconnect with the ground.

Visualize yourself grounding your energy and drawing strength from the earth.

● **Sensory Exploration:** As you walk to work or run errands, pay attention to the sensory details of your surroundings. Notice the scent of freshly cut grass, the warmth of the sun on your skin, or the sound of birds singing. Engage all your senses to appreciate the beauty of the natural world, even in an urban environment.

Remember, busy bee witches, even small steps can deepen your connection with nature. By incorporating these practices into your daily routine, you'll discover the magic that surrounds you and harness its power to enrich your busy bee life. Embrace the grounding energy of the earth, find inspiration in the ever-changing seasons, and weave the magic of nature into the very fabric of your witchcraft practice.

Chapter 12: Busy Bee Gardening Magic: Herbs & Flowers for Everyday Spells

Busy bee witches, rejoice! Even a tiny balcony or a simple window box can be transformed into a flourishing haven for herbs and flowers that not only beautify your space but also provide potent ingredients for your witchcraft practice. This chapter explores the concept of Busy Bee Gardening Magic, showcasing easy-to-grow plants and incorporating them into quick spells and rituals for the time-pressed witch.

From Seed to Spell: Cultivating Your Magical Garden Sanctuary:

Don't be discouraged by limited space! Container gardening is a perfect solution for busy bees who yearn to connect with the magic of plants. Here are some tips for creating your own witch's garden, no matter the size:

- **Pick Your Plants: Go Beyond the Basics:** Sure, classic herbs like basil (prosperity), lavender (peace), and rosemary (purification) are easy to grow and require minimal maintenance. But explore options that resonate with your specific needs! Here are some ideas to get you started:

  ○ **Protection:** Sage (cleansing and protection), Mugwort (psychic protection and dreamwork), Rue (banishing negativity).

○ **Healing:** Calendula (wounds and inflammation), Chamomile (calming and relaxation), Echinacea (immune system support).

○ **Love and Attraction:** Rose (love, beauty, and self-love), Jasmine (sensuality and attraction), Verbena (love and happiness).

○ **Prosperity:** Mint (abundance and growth), Bay leaf (success and achievement), Cinnamon (prosperity and good fortune).

● **Consider Your Climate:** Research plants that thrive in your specific climate zone. This will ensure your chosen herbs and flowers have the best chance of success, minimizing the time and effort you need to invest in their care.

● **Companion Planting:** Learn about companion planting, a technique where you plant certain herbs and flowers together to benefit each other. For example, borage deters pests from tomatoes, while nasturtiums attract beneficial insects that help control aphids. This can save you time and resources in the long run.

● **Container Magic:** Select pots or planters that suit your aesthetic taste and available space. **Think Outside the Box (Literally):** Don't be afraid to get creative! Upcycle old watering cans, colanders, or even shoes for a unique and personalized touch. Use hanging baskets for vertical gardening on balconies or patios. Research self-watering planters as an option to minimize watering needs, especially if you're truly a busy bee!

• **Planting and Care:** Research the specific needs of your chosen plants. Most herbs and flowers thrive with well-draining soil and regular watering. A quick internet search will provide detailed information on planting, sunlight requirements, and any specific care instructions for your chosen herbs and flowers. Remember, even busy bees can manage a thriving garden with a little planning!

Busy Bee Spells with Freshly Picked Magic:

Now that your miniature magical garden is flourishing, here are some quick spells and rituals you can perform using your homegrown bounty:

• **Protection Pouch:** Feeling the need for a little extra shielding energy? Snip some rosemary sprigs from your garden. Cleanse them under running water and allow them to dry completely. Place the dried rosemary in a small cloth pouch along with a pinch of salt (for purification) and a black tourmaline crystal (for grounding and protection). Carry this pouch with you throughout the day for a sense of security and protection.

• **Calming Bath Ritual:** After a long and stressful day, create a soothing bath infused with the calming essence of lavender. Harvest a few sprigs of lavender from your garden and tie them together with a ribbon to form a small bundle. Toss the lavender bundle into a hot bath and let it steep for a few minutes as the water absorbs the relaxing properties of the herb. Light a white candle or incense (if safe in your bathroom) and take some deep breaths, allowing the lavender's calming scent to wash away your worries.

- **Abundance Sigil Spell:** Intention to draw abundance into your life? Grow basil in your garden, a well-known herb associated with prosperity. Once a basil leaf has reached a good size, use a pen or marker to draw a sigil (a symbol imbued with your intention) onto the underside of the leaf. Visualize your abundance goals as you draw the sigil, infusing it with your intention. Place the sigil-drawn basil leaf on your windowsill under the light of a waxing moon (the period between the new moon and full moon) to charge it with lunar energy. Let the basil leaf dry completely, then crumble it up and add it to a potpourri mix or a sachet to carry with you, attracting abundance wherever you go.

Beyond the Basics: Herbal Incenses and Culinary Craft:

Busy bee witches can take their garden magic a step further! Here are some additional ways to incorporate your homegrown herbs into your practice:

- **DIY Herbal Incense:** Dry your excess herbs and create your own custom incense blends. Research herb combinations that correspond with your magical intent. For instance, lavender and chamomile can be combined for a calming incense blend, while rosemary and mint can create an energizing one. Tie the dried herbs together in small bundles or crumble them up and burn them in a heat-resistant dish, filling your space with their magical aromas. Consider using a charcoal disc specifically designed for burning incense, following safety guidelines to avoid smoke inhalation.

- **Culinary Craft with Magical Intent:** Cooking and baking can be a form of kitchen witchcraft. As you incorporate your homegrown herbs into your meals, infuse them with your intentions. Add a bay leaf (associated with protection) to your stew while visualizing shielding your loved ones from negativity. Sprinkle some thyme (known for strength and courage) into your morning smoothie as you set your intentions for a productive day. Every meal becomes a magical act, nourishing your body and spirit with the potent energy of your homegrown herbs.

Living with the Seasons: The Wheel of the Year in Your Garden
Busy bee witches can weave the magic of the changing seasons into their gardening practice. Here are some ideas to connect your garden to the eight Wiccan holidays (Sabbats) of the Wheel of the Year:

- **Yule (Winter Solstice):** Plant winter herbs like rosemary and thyme that thrive in cooler temperatures. Decorate your planters with festive pinecones or evergreen boughs.

- **Imbolc (February):** Start seeds indoors for herbs and flowers that will be transplanted outdoors in the spring. Celebrate the returning light by planting early-blooming bulbs like crocuses or snowdrops.

- **Ostara (Spring Equinox):** Plant a variety of herbs and flowers associated with spring, like chives (renewal), dill (protection), and pansies (rebirth). Celebrate the fertility of the earth by adding compost or fertilizer to your planters.

- **Beltane (May Day):** Plant herbs associated with love and protection, like rose (love), mugwort (psychic protection), and verbena (happiness). Decorate your garden with colorful streamers or ribbons to welcome the height of spring.

- **Litha (Summer Solstice):** Harvest herbs at their peak potency. Use your homegrown bounty in spells and rituals, or dry them for later use. Celebrate the abundance of the summer season by enjoying meals outdoors surrounded by your flourishing garden.

- **Lughnasadh (Lammas):** Harvest any remaining herbs and flowers from your garden. Preserve them by drying, infusing them into vinegar or oil, or freezing them for later use. Celebrate the first harvest by baking bread or creating a meal using ingredients from your garden.

- **Mabon (Autumn Equinox):** Plant cool-weather herbs like parsley and cilantro. Clear away spent plants and debris from your garden to prepare for winter. Reflect on the cycle of life, death, and rebirth as the seasons change.

- **Samhain (Halloween):** Harvest any remaining herbs for use in Samhain rituals or spells. Decorate your planters with gourds, pumpkins, or other seasonal elements. Celebrate the veil between the worlds thinning by honoring your ancestors or loved ones who have passed.

Remember, Busy Bee Witches, It's All About the Journey!

Creating a Busy Bee Gardening Magic practice doesn't have to be complicated or time-consuming. Even a small window box or a single pot on your balcony can be a source of immense joy and magical connection. Embrace the process of nurturing your plants, from planting the seeds to harvesting the bounty. Find joy in the vibrant colors, calming scents, and potent energy that your homegrown herbs and flowers bring to your life and practice.

Chapter 13: Busy Bee Nature Connection: Finding Magic in Every Moment

Busy bee witches, listen up! We all crave that connection to the natural world, the feeling of groundedness and peace that comes from being present in nature. But let's face it, carving out large chunks of time to explore forests or hike mountain trails can be a challenge in our jam-packed schedules. This chapter delves into the concept of Busy Bee Nature Connection, offering techniques for incorporating short bursts of nature connection into your day, even amidst the whirlwind of your busy life.

The Power of Nature's Embrace, Even in Squeezed-in Moments:

The benefits of connecting with nature are well-documented. Immersing yourself in the sights, sounds, and smells of the natural world reduces stress, improves mood, fosters a sense of well-being, and can even boost creativity. But for busy bees, the time to commune with nature often feels like a luxury we can't afford. Fear not! Here are some ways to sprinkle a touch of nature magic into your day, even amidst the whirlwind of your busy schedule:

- **The Mindful Minute:** Start small! Take a one-minute nature break throughout your day. Step outside, close your eyes, and focus on the sounds around you – birds chirping, leaves rustling in the breeze, the distant hum of traffic. Breathe deeply, feeling the air fill your lungs and the cool touch of wind on your skin. Even a minute of mindful presence in nature can have a profound effect on your mood and energy levels.

- **The Sensory Stroll:** Transform your walk to work, your lunchtime break, or even your errands into a nature exploration. Engage all your senses, truly experiencing the natural world around you, even if it's just a small park or a tree-lined street. Pay attention to the texture of the sidewalk beneath your feet, the different shades of green in the leaves overhead, the warmth of the sun on your skin, the scent of freshly cut grass, or the taste of a cool morning breeze. Notice the intricate details of a spiderweb glistening with dew, the playful dance of butterflies amongst the flowers, or the mesmerizing patterns formed by clouds drifting across a vast blue canvas. By actively engaging your senses, you'll be surprised by the hidden wonders waiting to be discovered, even in the most familiar urban environments.

- **The Window to Nature:** Don't have access to outdoor space? No problem! Even a window view can be a source of nature magic. Turn your window into a portal to the natural world. Take a few moments each day to gaze out the window, focusing on the trees swaying in the wind, the clouds drifting by, the birds flitting from branch to branch, or the playful antics of squirrels gathering nuts. Allow the natural world, even in this limited view, to bring a sense of calm and serenity into your day.

- **Nature Soundscapes:** Technology can be your friend when it comes to Busy Bee Nature Connection. During your commute or while taking a relaxing bath, listen to nature soundscapes. Immerse yourself in the calming sounds of a babbling brook, the rhythmic crashing of waves on the shore, or the gentle chirping of crickets in a summer meadow. These natural sounds can have a powerful effect on reducing stress and promoting relaxation, even if you can't be physically present in nature.

• **Urban Nature Exploration:** Busy bee witches who live in urban environments can still find pockets of nature to explore. Visit your local botanical garden, stroll through a community park, or simply find a quiet corner with a tree and a bench. Consider volunteering at a community garden or urban farm, connecting with nature while giving back to your local community.

Quick Ritual: A Mindful Walk for Connecting with the Natural World:

Busy bees, reclaim a sense of connection with the natural world through this simple mindful walk ritual.

• **Gather Your Supplies:** All you need is comfortable shoes and an open mind.

• **Set Your Intention:** Before you embark on your walk, take a moment to set your intention. Are you seeking relaxation and stress relief? Do you want to connect with the energy of a specific plant or tree? Perhaps you simply want to appreciate the beauty of nature. Holding an intention in your mind will focus your walk and deepen your connection.

• **Embark on Your Journey:** Find a park, nature trail, or even a quiet street with some greenery. As you walk, slow down and become present in the moment. Notice the details – the scent of pine needles, the texture of the bark on a tree, the sound of your own footsteps on the ground. Engage all your senses and truly experience the natural world around you.

• **Connect with a Plant or Tree:** If you feel drawn to a particular plant or tree, take a moment to connect with it. Pause for a moment, place your hand gently on its trunk or bark, feeling its energy. Whisper a silent greeting or express your gratitude for its presence. You might be surprised by the sense of calm and peace that washes over you as you connect with this living being.

• **End with Gratitude:** As you finish your walk, take a few moments to express your gratitude for nature's beauty and the sense of peace it brings you. Thank the specific plant or tree you connected with, and acknowledge the natural world for its role in your well-being.

• **Seal the Ritual:** Conclude your walk by taking a few deep breaths of fresh air. Visualize the calming energy of nature filling your body and spirit. Carry this sense of peace and connection with you throughout your day, allowing it to infuse your busy life with a touch of magic.

Remember, Busy Bee Witches, It's All About the Journey

Busy Bee Nature Connection isn't about grand adventures or escaping to remote wilderness. It's about weaving nature's magic into the fabric of your everyday life, no matter how ordinary it may seem. By incorporating these simple practices, you can cultivate a deep appreciation for the natural world, even in stolen moments. You'll find that even a brief connection with nature can have a profound impact on your mood, energy levels, and sense of well-being. So, busy bees, get out there, explore, connect, and weave the magic of nature into the extraordinary tapestry of your witchcraft practice.

Part 6: Busy Bee Magic for Modern Challenges

Life throws curveballs, even at the most organized busy bee witch! Part 6 tackles the challenges of maintaining your magical practice and well-being amidst stress and the demands of daily life. We'll explore how to integrate magic into your self-care routine, equipping you with tools to manage stress and cultivate inner peace. Discover how to:

Craft Magical Tools for Peace:

- **The Magic of Meditation:** In our fast-paced world, carving out time for meditation can feel like a luxury. However, even short bursts of mindfulness can have a profound impact on stress reduction. Here's a quick guided meditation specifically designed for busy bees:

  - Find a quiet corner in your home or office, free from distractions. Sit comfortably, with your back straight and feet flat on the floor. Close your eyes and take a few deep breaths, inhaling slowly through your nose and exhaling completely through your mouth.

  - Focus your attention on the sensation of your breath moving in and out of your body. Notice the rise and fall of your chest with each breath. If your mind wanders, gently guide your attention back to your breath, without judgment.

○ Visualize a calming image – a serene beach, a tranquil forest, or a gentle waterfall. Allow yourself to be enveloped by this peaceful image, feeling a sense of calm washing over you.

○ Continue for just 5-10 minutes, or as long as you have time. When you're ready, gently bring your awareness back to the room, wiggling your fingers and toes. Take a few deep breaths before opening your eyes, carrying the sense of peace with you throughout your day.

● **Crystal Allies for Stress Relief:** Crystals hold powerful energetic properties that can aid us in managing stress. Here are some crystals that can be incorporated into your self-care routine:

○ Amethyst: Known for its calming and stress-reducing properties. Carry a piece of amethyst in your pocket throughout the day or place it on your desk at work to promote serenity.

○ Lepidolite: Promotes emotional balance and reduces anxiety. Hold a piece of lepidolite during meditation or place it under your pillow for a restful night's sleep.

○ Selenite: Cleanses negative energy and promotes feelings of peace and tranquility. Place a selenite wand in your workspace to create a calming atmosphere.

● **Moon Magic for Busy Bees:** Don't underestimate the power of the moon's phases to enhance your self-care practice. During the calming energy of the waning moon, take a detox bath infused with Epsom salts and cleansing herbs like rosemary or sage. Focus on letting go of stress and negativity as the moon wanes. Conversely, harness the invigorating energy of the waxing moon to create a self-care ritual that sets intentions for growth and personal empowerment.

Embrace Busy Bee Self-Care Magic:

Self-care isn't a luxury; it's a necessity for busy bee witches! Weaving magic into your self-care routine allows you to nurture your spirit, promote self-love, and recharge your energy. Here are some ideas:

- **The Magical Bath Ritual:** After a long and demanding day, create a luxurious bath infused with magical intentions to rejuvenate your mind, body, and spirit.

  ○ Gather your tools: Epsom salts for relaxation, essential oils for their specific properties (lavender for calmness, jasmine for self-love, etc.), a few candles, and a selection of healing herbs (chamomile for peace, rose petals for self-love).

  ○ Light your candles and run a warm bath, adding Epsom salts and your chosen essential oils.

  ○ While the bath fills, brew a cup of calming herbal tea. As you prepare your tea, visualize your intention for the bath – washing away stress, promoting self-love, or simply letting go of the day's worries.

  ○ Once the bath is ready, add your herbs and climb in. Sip your tea while soaking in the calming water, allowing the essential oils and herbals to work their magic.

○ Close your eyes and focus on your breath, visualizing the negative energy and stress dissolving away. Imagine yourself feeling refreshed, rejuvenated, and full of self-love.

○ After your bath, wrap yourself in a cozy towel and spend some quiet time reading, meditating, or simply resting.

• **Quick Sigil Spell for Self-Care:** Feeling overwhelmed by a busy schedule? Create a sigil (a symbol imbued with your intention) for self-care. On a small piece of paper, draw a symbol that represents self-care to you – a heart, a flower, or a peaceful image. As you draw, visualize feelings of peace, relaxation, and prioritizing your well-being. Fold the paper and tuck it into your pocket or place it under your pillow as a reminder to take care of yourself.

• **Kitchen Witchery for Busy Bees:** Food is a powerful source of energy, and incorporating magical intention into your meals can be a delightful form of self-care. When you're feeling stressed or depleted, create a nourishing meal infused with herbs associated with well-being. Add a sprig of rosemary (associated with purification and mental clarity) to your chicken soup, or sprinkle some rose petals (known for self-love and emotional healing) into your herbal tea. As you prepare and consume your food, visualize the herbs' beneficial properties nourishing your body and spirit.

Remember, busy bee witches, self-care is a practice, not a destination. By incorporating these simple magical tools and rituals into your daily routine, you can create a haven of peace and self-love amidst the whirlwind of your busy life. You'll be amazed at how these small acts of magic can have a profound impact on your well-being and allow you to approach your craft and your life with renewed energy and a sense of inner peace.

Chapter 14: Busy Bee Stress Management: Magical Tools for Peace

Busy bee witches, we all know the feeling – that constant hum of stress buzzing beneath the surface, threatening to overwhelm us. But fear not! This chapter equips you with magical tools for peace, offering techniques and practices to incorporate magic into stress reduction and cultivate a sense of calm amidst the whirlwind of your busy life.

Taming the Bees: Magical Techniques for Stress Management:

Stress can be a major energy drain for busy bees. Left unchecked, it can impact our health, well-being, and even our magical practice. Luckily, witchcraft offers a powerful arsenal of tools to combat stress and cultivate inner peace. Here are some ways to infuse magic into your stress management routine:

- **The Power of Protection:** Feeling overwhelmed? Create a simple magical shield to deflect negativity and stress. Light a white candle, symbolizing purity and protection. Visualize a white light surrounding you, enveloping you in a bubble of calm energy. Whisper a charm or affirmation, such as "Peace surrounds me, stress dissipates," to further empower your visualization. Repeat this simple ritual whenever you feel the need for a moment of protection and calm.

- **Sigil Magic for Serenity:** Sigils are powerful symbols infused with your intention. For stress management, create a sigil representing peace and serenity. There are many online resources and books that offer guidance on sigil creation. Once you've created your sigil, draw it on a piece of paper or carve it into a candle. Meditate on the feeling of peace and calmness as you focus on the sigil. Light the candle (if you carved it) or carry the sigil with you as a reminder of your intention to stay calm and centered.

• **Moon Magic for Stress Relief:** The moon's cycles can be powerful allies in stress management. During the waning moon (the period between the full moon and new moon), when energy is naturally releasing, perform rituals or meditations focused on letting go of stress and negativity. Light a blue candle (associated with calmness) and write down your worries on a piece of paper. Visualize the worries burning away with the blue candle flame. Rip the paper into small pieces and release them, either outside in the wind or by flushing them down the toilet with the intention of letting them go with the waning moon.

• **Aromatherapy for Anxiety Relief:** Essential oils can be powerful tools for stress management. Lavender oil is well-known for its calming properties. Diffuse a few drops of lavender oil in your workspace or bedroom, or dab a diluted solution (a few drops mixed with carrier oil like almond oil) on your wrists or temples to promote relaxation. Cedarwood oil is another grounding oil that can help to ease anxiety and promote restful sleep. Diffuse it at night or add a few drops to your bath.

• **Infuse Your Cleaning with Calming Magic:** Chores can be a major source of stress for busy bees. Transform your cleaning routine into a mini-ritual for stress relief. Light a green candle (associated with growth and new beginnings) as you start cleaning. Play calming music and focus on the repetitive motions of cleaning as a form of meditation. Imagine yourself clearing away not just physical clutter, but also emotional clutter and negativity from your space.

Quick Meditation: A Short Guided Meditation for Busy Bees: Don't have a lot of time? This short guided meditation can help you find a moment of peace and quiet amidst your busy schedule:

- **Find a Quiet Spot:** Take a few minutes to find a quiet corner, close your eyes, and take a few deep breaths.

- **Ground Yourself:** Imagine yourself rooted to the ground like a strong tree. Feel your connection to the earth through your feet.

- **Visualize Calmness:** Imagine a calming scene – a peaceful beach, a quiet forest, or a serene meadow. Focus on the details of the scene – the sound of waves lapping at the shore, the rustling of leaves in the breeze, the warmth of the sun on your skin.

- **Release Tension:** With each breath, visualize stress and tension leaving your body. Imagine it as a dark cloud floating away from you.

- **Return Refreshed:** After a few minutes, slowly bring your awareness back to the present moment. Take a few more deep breaths and open your eyes, feeling refreshed and centered.

Crystal Magic: Using Crystals for Calming and Grounding:

Crystals are powerful tools for stress management in the world of witchcraft. Here are some crystals that can be particularly helpful for busy bees:

- **Amethyst:** This beautiful purple crystal is known for its calming and protective properties. Carry a piece of amethyst in your pocket or place it on your desk to promote relaxation.

- **Black Tourmaline:** This grounding stone is a shield against negativity, promoting a sense of calm and security. Meditate with a piece of black tourmaline to absorb and release stress.

- **Lepidolite:** This calming stone promotes emotional balance and reduces anxiety. Place a piece of lepidolite under your pillow to promote restful sleep and reduce stress-related insomnia.

- **Smoky Quartz:** This grounding stone helps to dispel negativity and anxiety. Carry a piece of smoky quartz in your pocket or place it at your workspace to create a sense of calm and focus.

Remember, Busy Bee Witches, Self-Care is Key:
Stress management isn't just about magical tools and techniques; it's also about prioritizing self-care. Make sure you're getting enough sleep, eating healthy foods, and exercising regularly. These healthy habits will provide a strong foundation for your magical stress management practice.

- **Listen to Your Body:** Your body is a wise teacher. Pay attention to the physical signs of stress, such as headaches, muscle tension, or difficulty sleeping. When you recognize these signs, take action! Don't wait until you're overwhelmed. Utilize your magical tools and self-care practices to address your stress before it gets out of control.

● **Build a Support System:** No busy bee witch is an island! Having a strong support system of friends, family, or fellow witches can be a lifesaver during stressful times. Talk to your loved ones about your stress and seek their support. You might be surprised at how much a listening ear or a helping hand can alleviate your burdens.

● **Celebrate Your Victories:** Even small victories in the battle against stress deserve to be celebrated! Acknowledge your progress and take pride in your efforts to manage your well-being. Celebrating your successes will keep you motivated and focused on your journey to a calmer, more peaceful you.

By incorporating these magical tools and techniques into your daily routine, busy bee witches, you can transform stress from a relentless foe into a manageable challenge. Remember, self-care is not a luxury – it's a necessity for a thriving magical practice and a fulfilling life.

Chapter 15: Busy Bee Self-Care Magic: Rejuvenating Your Spirit

Busy bee witches, we all know the importance of self-care. But carving out time for elaborate rituals can feel like a luxury amidst the whirlwind of our busy schedules. Fear not! This chapter explores the concept of Busy Bee Self-Care Magic, offering simple spells and rituals for self-love and rejuvenation that are easy to integrate into your daily routine, even amidst the constant buzz.

Blooming Where You're Planted: Self-Care for the Time-Pressed Witch:

Self-care isn't about self-indulgence; it's about tending to your physical, emotional, and spiritual well-being so you can show up for yourself and your practice with renewed energy. For busy bees, self-care needs to be efficient and impactful. Here are some ways to sprinkle a touch of magic into your self-care routine:

- **Moon Water Magic:** The moon's energy can be harnessed for self-care purposes. Under the light of a full moon (associated with completeness and culmination), fill a glass jar or bowl with water. Add a few drops of essential oil that resonates with your self-care intentions – lavender for relaxation, rose for self-love, or citrus for a mood boost. Let the water sit under the full moon's light for several hours or overnight. In the morning, use the moon water in your bath, mist your face throughout the day, or even add a few drops to your water bottle for an extra dose of lunar magic.

● **The Power of Positive Affirmations:** Words have power, and positive affirmations can be a simple yet powerful tool for self-care. Start your day by repeating affirmations that resonate with your needs. "I am strong and capable," "I am worthy of love and happiness," or "I release stress and embrace peace" are just a few examples. Write them down on sticky notes and place them around your mirror, desk, or anywhere you'll see them throughout the day to serve as a constant reminder.

● **Declutter for Inner Peace:** Physical clutter can contribute to feelings of overwhelm and anxiety. Dedicate a few minutes each day to declutter your workspace or living area. Light a white candle (associated with purity and cleansing) and visualize negativity and stress leaving your space as you declutter. Donating unwanted items to charity adds a layer of generosity to your self-care practice. A tidy space promotes a clear mind and a sense of calm.

● **The Tech Witch's Self-Care Sanctuary:** Busy bees can leverage technology to enhance their self-care routines. Create a playlist filled with calming music or nature sounds to unwind after a long day. Download a meditation app to sneak in a few minutes of mindfulness practice during your commute or lunch break. There are even apps specifically designed for self-care, offering guided meditations, breathing exercises, and journaling prompts – all at your fingertips!

Beyond the Bath: Self-Care Rituals for Every Busy Bee:
While a luxurious bath can be a wonderful self-care practice, busy bees don't always have the time to indulge. Here are some additional self-care rituals that can be done in just a few minutes:

- **Morning Meditation:** Start your day with a short meditation practice. Sit comfortably, close your eyes, and focus on your breath. Even five minutes of mindful meditation can help to reduce stress and promote feelings of calm and focus.

- **Power Pose Power Up:** Feeling overwhelmed? Take a power stance! Stand tall with your feet shoulder-width apart, hands on hips, and chin held high. This power pose has been shown to boost confidence and reduce stress hormones. Hold the pose for a few minutes while visualizing yourself feeling strong and capable.

- **Digital Detox:** In our constantly connected world, it's easy to feel overwhelmed by technology. Schedule regular digital detox breaks throughout your day. Silence your phone notifications, put away your laptop, and simply be present in the moment. Take a walk in nature, read a book, or spend time with loved ones. You'll be surprised at how refreshed you feel after a break from the digital world.

- **Nourish Your Body:** Self-care isn't just about bubble baths and meditation; it's also about taking care of your physical well-being. Fuel your body with nutritious foods and stay hydrated throughout the day. Getting enough sleep is also essential for self-care. Aim for seven to eight hours of sleep each night to wake up feeling refreshed and energized.

Remember, busy bee witches, self-care is essential for maintaining your energy and well-being. By incorporating these simple spells and rituals into your routine, you can create pockets of self-love and rejuvenation amidst the hustle and bustle of your daily life. Blessed be!

Bath Ritual: A Luxurious Bath Ritual with Magical Intentions

Sometimes, a luxurious bath is exactly what the busy bee witch needs! Transform your bathroom into a magical sanctuary with this simple yet rejuvenating bath ritual.

Gather Your Supplies:

- Light a few candles (choose colors that resonate with your intention – lavender or blue for relaxation, pink for self-love, or orange for creativity).

- Draw a warm bath and add a cup of Epsom salts (known for their detoxifying properties) and a few drops of your favorite essential oil.

- Prepare a cup of herbal tea or calming beverage to sip during your bath.

Set Your Intention:

Before stepping into the bath, take a moment to set your intention. Are you seeking relaxation after a long day? Do you want to clear away negative energy and promote self-love? Holding an intention in your mind will focus your bath ritual and amplify its magical effects.

Immerse Yourself in Magic:

Sink into the warm, soothing water and close your eyes. Visualize the stresses and worries of the day melting away like bubbles. Imagine the Epsom salts and essential oils drawing out negativity and replacing it with your desired energy. Sip your tea and allow the warmth and calming scents to fill your senses.

Gratitude and Affirmations:

As you soak, take a moment to express gratitude for your body and all that it allows you to do. Repeat a positive affirmation that resonates with your intention. "I am strong and capable," "I am worthy of love and happiness," or "I am releasing stress and embracing peace" are just a few examples.

Seal the Ritual:

After enjoying your bath, take a few deep breaths and visualize yourself feeling refreshed and rejuvenated. Step out of the bath, pat yourself dry, and wrap yourself in a cozy towel or robe. Carry the feeling of peace and self-love with you throughout the rest of your day.

Remember, busy bee witches, self-care is a gift you give yourself. Make it a priority, and watch your well-being and magical practice flourish!

Bonus Tip: Enhance your bath ritual with a touch of music! Create a playlist filled with calming spa music, nature sounds, or chants that resonate with your intention. Let the music further elevate the magical experience and transport you to a place of tranquility.

Bonus Content: More For Your Busy Bee Witch Toolkit

You've unlocked the secrets to integrating magic into your busy bee life! But the journey doesn't stop here. This bonus section provides additional resources to empower you on your magical path.

- Glossary of Busy Bee Witchcraft Terms: Brush up on key terms and concepts used throughout the book with our handy glossary.

- Sample Busy Bee Weekly Schedule: Feeling overwhelmed about fitting magic into your already packed schedule? We've got you covered! This sample weekly schedule provides a framework for integrating magical practices into your everyday routine, demonstrating how even small bursts of magic can make a big difference.

- Printable Spell Cards: Create your own personalized deck of spells and rituals for easy reference! This section provides instructions and templates for crafting printable cards with quick spells and rituals that resonate with your needs and intentions.

Consider this bonus section your personal toolkit, filled with resources to enhance your busy bee witchcraft practice and keep the magic flowing throughout your life.

Glossary of Busy Bee Witchcraft Terms:

This glossary provides definitions for key terms used throughout the book to empower busy bee witches on their magical journeys:

- **Busy Bee Witch:** A witch who leads a busy and active lifestyle but still prioritizes incorporating witchcraft practices into their daily routine.

- **Crystal Magic:** Utilizing the power of crystals for various magical purposes.

- **Declutter:** Removing unwanted or unnecessary items from a space.

- **Essential Oils:** Concentrated plant extracts with various therapeutic properties.

- **Full Moon Water:** Water charged under the light of a full moon, believed to hold potent magical properties.

- **Grounding:** The act of connecting your energy with the earth.

- **Intention:** The focused purpose or desired outcome of a spell or ritual.

- **Moon Magic:** Utilizing the different phases of the moon's cycle for magical purposes.

- **Self-Care:** Practices that nourish your physical, emotional, and spiritual well-being.

- **Sigil:** A symbol infused with magical intention.

This glossary provides a starting point for busy bee witches. As you delve deeper into your witchcraft journey, you'll encounter a wider range of terminology. Embrace the exploration, trust your intuition, and remember, blessed be!

Sample Busy Bee Weekly Schedule:

Being a busy bee witch doesn't mean sacrificing your magical practice! This sample schedule demonstrates how to integrate quick bursts of witchcraft into your everyday life, even amidst a packed week. Remember, this is just a template – feel free to adjust it to fit your specific work hours, commitments, and personal preferences.

Monday:

- **6:00 AM - 6:15 AM: Morning Meditation & Sigil Activation:** Start your week with a short meditation to focus your intentions. Sit comfortably, close your eyes, and take a few deep breaths. Imagine a calming white light filling your body, washing away any lingering stress from the weekend. Then, visualize your sigil for abundance (created during a previous ritual) glowing with energy as you set your intentions for a prosperous week. See the sigil pulsating with vibrant light, attracting opportunities and success throughout the week ahead.

- **7:00 PM - 7:15 PM: Quick Cleansing Ritual:** After a busy day, perform a simple cleansing ritual to release negativity and promote peace. Light a white candle (associated with purity) and run your hands through the smoke, visualizing negativity leaving your body and spirit. Imagine the smoke carrying away any anxieties or frustrations you encountered during the day. Breathe deeply, feeling lighter and more centered as the cleansing smoke washes over you.

Tuesday:

● **12:00 PM - 12:15 PM: Lunchtime Nature Walk:** During your lunch break, take a short walk in a nearby park or green space. Engage your senses, focusing on the sights, sounds, and smells of nature. Notice the vibrant colors of the flowers, the calming murmur of a nearby stream, or the gentle rustle of leaves in the breeze. This mindful walk serves as a quick nature connection and a way to de-stress in the middle of the day. Let the natural world recharge your batteries and bring a sense of peace amidst the bustle of your work week.

● **8:00 PM - 8:15 PM: Crystal Grid for Protection:** Before bed, set up a simple crystal grid for protection using black tourmaline crystals (known for their protective properties). Place the crystals in a grid pattern on your nightstand, visualizing a shield of protection around you as you sleep. See the black tourmaline crystals absorbing any negativity that might try to enter your space, ensuring a peaceful and restful night's sleep.

Wednesday:

● **5:00 AM - 5:10 AM: Sun Salutations & Gratitude:** Start your day with a few sun salutations to energize your body and spirit. Stretch your limbs towards the rising sun, feeling its warmth invigorate you for the day ahead. End your morning routine with a short gratitude practice, expressing appreciation for the blessings in your life, big or small. Be thankful for your health, your loved ones, and the opportunities that await you. Gratitude sets a positive tone for the day and reminds you of the abundance already present in your life.

● **10:00 PM - 10:05 PM: Moon Water Creation (Optional):** If there's a full moon this week, leave a glass or bowl of water outside under the moonlight for a few hours to create moon water. This moon water can be used for cleansing, charging objects, or in spells for specific intentions. Intentionally infuse the water with the moon's potent energy, creating a magical tool to enhance your future rituals and practices.

Thursday:

● **7:30 AM - 7:35 AM: Aromatherapy for Focus:** Diffuse a few drops of peppermint oil in your workspace to enhance focus and concentration as you start your workday. The invigorating scent of peppermint will help you clear your mind and approach your tasks with renewed focus.

● **6:00 PM - 6:15 PM: Kitchen Witchcraft:** Infuse your dinner with a touch of magic! Add a bay leaf (associated with protection) to your pot of stew while visualizing shielding your loved ones from negativity. See the bay leaf acting as a magical charm, imbuing your meal with protective energy. As you cook and share this meal with loved ones, know that you're not just nourishing their bodies, but also their well-being.

Friday:

- **1:00 PM - 1:15 PM: Mindful Eating Meditation:** Take a few minutes before your lunch break to center yourself. Focus on your breath and appreciate the food you're about to consume. Give thanks for the bounty of the earth and the nourishment it provides. This mindful eating practice promotes gratitude and digestion. Savor each bite, allowing your body to fully absorb the nutrients and energy from your meal.

- **8:00 PM - 8:30 PM: Digital Detox & Positive Affirmations:** Unplug from technology for a half-hour before bed. Turn off your phone notifications, silence your computer, and simply be present in the moment. Light a candle (choose a color that resonates with your needs – lavender for relaxation, or orange for creativity) and spend a few minutes journaling, reflecting on the week's experiences and setting intentions for the weekend ahead. Write down a few positive affirmations to empower yourself, repeating them aloud to solidify your intentions for a positive and magical weekend.

Weekend:

This is your time to delve deeper into your magical practice, recharge your batteries, and explore your witchcraft with more freedom. Here are some ideas to get you started:

- **Spend time in nature:** Immerse yourself in the natural world, a powerful source of energy and inspiration. Go for a hike, visit a local park, or simply sit in your backyard and connect with the earth.

- **Try a new spell or ritual:** Weekends are a perfect time to experiment with new spells or rituals that you might not have time for during the week. Explore a new area of witchcraft that interests you, or revisit an old favorite.

● **Create a magical self-care ritual:** Take some time to pamper yourself and create a self-care ritual infused with magic. Draw a relaxing bath with essential oils and herbs, light some candles, and meditate on your intentions for self-love and rejuvenation.

● **Connect with your coven or fellow witches:** If you have a coven, schedule a gathering for the weekend. Spend time practicing magic together, sharing experiences, and supporting each other on your witchcraft journeys. If you don't have a coven, consider joining an online witch community or seeking out other local witches to connect with.

Remember, busy bee witches, this is just a sample schedule. The key is to find ways to weave magic into the fabric of your everyday life, even amidst the whirlwind.

Printable Spell Cards: Create Your Own Busy Bee Witch Arsenal!

Busy bee witches, here's your chance to create a personalized deck of printable spell cards for easy reference! This section provides templates and examples to inspire you to craft quick and effective spells and rituals that you can integrate into your daily routine.

Materials:

- Cardstock or thick printer paper
- Scissors (optional: paper cutter for even cuts)
- Printer
- Pens or markers (optional for personalization)
- Corner rounder (optional)

Instructions:

1. Copy the template below. You can also create your own design using a word processing program or drawing software.
2. Print the template on cardstock or thick printer paper.
3. Cut out the cards using scissors or a paper cutter.
4. (Optional) Use a corner rounder to create rounded corners on your cards for a more polished look.
5. Fill out the cards with your chosen spells and rituals. Refer to the examples below for inspiration, or create your own based on your needs and intentions.
6. Keep your deck of spell cards handy – on your desk, bulletin board, or even in your purse or bag – for easy access

throughout the day.

Template:
(Front of Card)
Spell Name: ___________________________
Intention: ___________________________
(Back of Card)
Instructions: ___________________________
Optional: Notes or Substitutions ___________________________
Examples:

- **Spell Name:** Morning Focus Boost

- **Intention:** Enhance concentration and clarity of mind at the start of the day.

- **Instructions:** Light a yellow candle (associated with mental focus) and repeat a positive affirmation like "I am focused and clear-headed" three times. Visualize a beam of yellow light energizing your mind and promoting concentration.

- **Notes:** Substitute a yellow crystal (such as citrine) for the candle if desired.

- **Spell Name:** Cleansing Commute Commute

- **Intention:** Release negativity and stress accumulated during your commute.

- **Instructions:** As you travel (by car, bus, train, etc.), take a few deep breaths and visualize a white light surrounding you. See the white light cleansing away any negativity or stress you picked up throughout the day.

- **Notes:** If possible, open a window or fan to circulate the cleansing energy.

- **Spell Name:** Tech Detox Tranquility

- **Intention:** Promote peace and relaxation before bed by disconnecting from technology.

- **Instructions:** One hour before bedtime, turn off all electronic devices (phone, computer, TV). Light a calming blue candle (associated with peace) and read a book, take a relaxing bath, or practice mindfulness meditation.

- **Spell Name:** Weekend Abundance Ritual

- **Intention:** Attract prosperity and abundance during the weekend.

- **Instructions:** Gather a bay leaf (associated with success) and a green candle (associated with abundance). Light the candle and hold the bay leaf in your hands, visualizing green light radiating from the candle and infusing the bay leaf with your intention of prosperity. Place the bay leaf in your wallet or purse to carry the energy of abundance with you throughout the weekend.

Remember, busy bee witches, the key is to personalize your spells and rituals to fit your unique needs and preferences. Get creative, have fun, and weave the magic of witchcraft into the fabric of your busy life! Blessed be!

As you close this book, dear Busy Bee Witch, hold onto the knowledge that you are a potent force. You've unlocked the secrets to weaving magic into the very fabric of your bustling life, transforming the ordinary into the extraordinary. Remember, the path of Busy Bee

Witchcraft isn't about achieving some unattainable ideal. It's about savoring the present moment, embracing the chaos with a sprinkle of enchantment, and integrating magical practices into the nooks and crannies of your already overflowing schedule.

There will be days when you stumble, days when your to-do list seems to mock your best intentions. Don't let those moments discourage you. The beauty of Busy Bee Witchcraft lies in its adaptability. It's okay to miss a meditation session or have a less-than-stellar attempt at a sigil. Celebrate your victories, no matter how small they seem, and learn valuable lessons from your missteps. Most importantly, trust your gut instinct. Allow your magical practice to flow and evolve alongside you, just like the ever-changing seasons.

Remember, dear witch, you are not alone on this path. There's a vibrant community of Busy Bee Witches out there, buzzing with energy and inspiration. Share your experiences, both triumphs and challenges, with fellow practitioners. Learn from their journeys and offer your own insights in return. Together, you can create a world where magic isn't relegated to dusty tomes and faraway lands. It can be a vibrant thread woven into the tapestry of your everyday life, a source of strength, and a reminder of the extraordinary power you hold within. So go forth, Busy Bee Witch, and keep the magic buzzing! Blessed be!

Don't miss out!

Visit the website below and you can sign up to receive emails whenever Emilee Avink publishes a new book. There's no charge and no obligation.

https://books2read.com/r/B-A-OHAFB-UNOID

BOOKS 2 READ

Connecting independent readers to independent writers.

Did you love *Buzzing with Magic: Quick & Effective Witchcraft for Busy Bees*? Then you should read *The Healing Table: Crystal-Infused Meals*[1] by Emilee Avink!

Unleash the Magic in Your Meals with A Pinch of Magic, A Spark of Crystal

Ever wondered how to add a little enchantment to your everyday cooking?

A Pinch of Magic, A Spark of Crystal is your guide to the fascinating world of crystal-infused cuisine. This book takes you on a culinary adventure, where you'll discover how to:

Harness the power of crystals to infuse your food with specific energies, promoting everything from love and abundance to clarity and detoxification.

---

1. https://books2read.com/u/4XNZL7

2. https://books2read.com/u/4XNZL7

Craft delicious and magical meals aligned with the phases of the moon, maximizing the power of your intentions.

Create crystal-infused waters, oils, and vinegars, adding a touch of magic to every step of your cooking process.

Design stunning crystal grids to activate your dishes and weave powerful intentions into your meals.

Brew mystical elixirs for specific needs, promoting well-being and a touch of enchantment.

This comprehensive guide includes:

A detailed exploration of crystal correspondences to match the perfect crystal to your culinary creations.

Dozens of mouthwatering recipes for breakfast, lunch, dinner, and dessert, all infused with the magic of crystals.

Essential information on crystal care and maintenance, ensuring your magical tools stay potent.

Kitchen witchery rituals to weave enchantment into your daily meals.

A Pinch of Magic, A Spark of Crystal is more than a cookbook; it's an invitation to transform your kitchen into a sacred space. Embark on this magical journey and discover the power to elevate your meals from ordinary to extraordinary!

Also by Emilee Avink

Embracing the Witch's Shadow: A Guide to Transformation and Self-Discovery: Unlocking the Secrets of Witchcraft, Healing and Personal Empowerment

Where Two Worlds Collide

The Infinite Loop: A Time Traveler's Search for Love

Whispers of the Guardian: Haleema's Legacy

The Pot of Plenty: Stretching Your Dollar with 50 Delicious Rice and Bean Dishes

Description for Nine Lives of Magic: Working with Your Feline Familiar

Once Upon a Feast: Fairytale Treats for Little Chefs

The Glitching Grimoire: A Tech Witch's Guide to Digital Spellcraft

The Healing Table: Crystal-Infused Meals

Buzzing with Magic: Quick & Effective Witchcraft for Busy Bees

The Witch's Daily Cup: Rituals and Recipes for Coffee Magic

www.ingramcontent.com/pod-product-compliance
Lightning Source LLC
Chambersburg PA
CBHW031332160726
47993CB00002B/640